THREE TIMES LUCKY

THREE TIMES LUCKY
JIMMY JEWEL

Enigma Books

First published in Great Britain in 1982 by Enigma Books,
an imprint of Severn House Publishers Limited,
4 Brook Street, London W1Y 1AA.

British Library Cataloguing in Publication Data

Jewel, Jimmy
　　Three times lucky.
　　1. Jewel, Jimmy　　2. Comedians—Great Britain
　　Biography
　　I. Title
　　791'.092'4　　PN2598.J/
　　ISBN 0-7278-3005-8

110 05

Phototypeset by Tradespools Limited, Frome, Somerset

Printed and bound in Great Britain by
Anchor Press Ltd, and bound by Wm. Brendon & Son Ltd,
both of Tiptree, Essex

I would like the following poem 'Rondel' to serve as a
dedication to my family. It was translated into English by
Sir Henry Newbolt from the French of Wenceslas,
Duke of Brabant and Luxembourg who died in 1384.

Long ago to thee I gave
Body, soul, and all I have—
   Nothing in the world I keep:

All that in return I crave
Is that thou accept the slave
Long ago to thee I gave—
   Body, soul, and all I have.

Had I more to share or save,
I would give as give the brave,
   Stooping not to part the heap;
Long ago to thee I gave
Body, soul, and all I have—
   Nothing in the world I keep.

The Publishers would like to thank Peter Newbolt for his kind permission to reproduce the poem 'Rondel' on the dedicatory page.

Part One

One

The Alhambra Theatre, Barnsley, 1917 ... My father, James Marsh, was in a spot of trouble. He couldn't find a midget for his panto. In December midgets were always in heavy demand for circuses and Christmas shows. He had tried advertising in the trade papers but with no luck. He looked at me. At five, I was small enough and I knew a bit about the business. I'd been involved virtually since the womb, my mother having fed my father his lines on stage when she was pregnant, up until a fortnight before I was born. I could paint a bit of scenery and I'd seen how he made the traps with springs on the doors so that, when you dived through, they closed quickly after you. He had shown me how the acrobats did it and, after a few attempts, I could do it. He decided to take a chance.

He was playing the part of Billy Crusoe in Robinson Crusoe and I was to take the part of a little red devil. He had built a trick set, a ship's cabin that rocked in heavy seas. In the scene where I was to appear, he was supposed to be drunk, hallucinating in the rocking cabin with a dose of the DTs. That was me, a five year old DT, wearing a red leotard and a pair of little horns. All I had to do was spring onto the stage through a trap-door—a lion's leap, it was called—followed by a roll-over.

By opening night he must have thought I could manage it. I mean, you don't need a lot of intelligence to dive head first through a trap-door. I got into my leotard, adjusted my horns and crouched on the slider—the false piece of flooring two feet beneath the stage. Three stage hands were ready to heave on weighted ropes and propel me up through the six-feet-square gap on to the stage—where I would scare the wits out of Billy Crusoe and, or so we hoped, the audience.

Unfortunately I wasn't standing in the centre of the chalk mark. Maybe it was stage-fright or something, I don't know. But when I got my cue and the ropes were pulled I hit my left shoulder on the stage floor and rolled onto the deck squealing with pain. I had broken my shoulder and I was off before I had begun: away, in my horns, to hospital.

Later some smart-Alec said something about this being my first break in show business: very amusing, but I didn't laugh at the time and neither did my father. He never did find his midget. . . .

Two

I was born on 4 December 1912 in my Grandma Driver's bed in Pittsmore, Sheffield. My father was playing the Theatre Royal, Bury, and when he heard the news, he jumped into his new Darraque car and set off over the Pennines to see me. It must have been quite a journey. The Snake Head Pass is a dodgy road especially in winter, full of twists and bends and hazards. It's not difficult to go clean over the edge and my father was not the best of drivers.

I'm told, though, that he was in an excellent mood. He had tried out a new sketch on the Bury audience, and apparently it had gone down well. He was a master at building trick scenery and at that time he was finding his feet as a performer. He must have been well pleased with himself: a success at Bury and a son in Sheffield. He had also just given himself a new stage name: James A. Jewel. I don't know where he got the idea of Jewel from but he thought it had a nice ring to it. Jewel looked better on the bills than Marsh.

He arrived (in one piece) at my grandma's house to be reunited with my mother. She had left the show two weeks' earlier and it was probably their longest separation. There and then, he and my mother decided that I would be named after him. James Arthur Thomas Jewel Marsh, to be baptised into the Church of England at the parish church, Healey, Sheffield.

He spent the night at Pittsmore and drove back the next day for the evening performance. Three weeks later my mother joined him and for the first two years of my life, until the First World War, I was looked after by my Grandma Driver, with my parents coming to see me on Sundays.

I remember it as a classically happy childhood. Any tears or tantrums or childish miseries I might have had have been forgotten. I vaguely recall my grandma as a frail old woman with great energy, but I don't remember the house. My earliest recollections of Sheffield are of the house at 131 Cobden View Road, Crookes, which my father rented. I remember it as a big house on a hill, the only double-fronted house in the street. There was a big drawing room with an aspidistra and a table where I was stretched out once to have my adenoids removed. There was Chat the cat who slept in the oven. Chat grew old and my father tried to drown him in a pot, but Chat wasn't having it. I remember seeing his little pink nose poking out under the lid. My father couldn't do it. Chat got a reprieve and won himself another year or so.

Looking back at old faded photographs, I see myself with a mass of wavy hair and a sailor suit. The hair didn't last long. It started to go thin at sixteen and was mostly gone by the time I was twenty-two. I was surrounded in those days by aunts and uncles. In one picture, Grandad Marsh stands on the right, a big man with white hair and moustache. He worked the gallery box office at the old Hippodrome, Sheffield. For fifteen years he fiddled the take and made enough to buy a pub, the Mail Coach. There was a big concert room in the pub where my father, as a kid, would give concert parties for the other kids. I don't remember much about Grandad Marsh except for his moustache.

My father dominates all the photographs; a stocky, powerful man, straight-backed, trying to look serious for the photographer. His formal pose belied his nature. He was a warm, affectionate man, a humorous man and at times a bit of a prankster. He was a natural comedian but he took his work seriously: a perfectionist who worked hard at his major talent of designing and making trick scenery.

He started out his professional life as a scenic artist working for a man called McCulloch who had a studio off the Moor in Sheffield. I don't know where or how he met Gertrude, my mother, just that they were both twenty-one when they married in Sheffield in 1902. My sister Mona was born a year later, dark and pretty like my mother with her mother's porcelain complexion.

Before I was born, my mother and father toured the north of England with my father's sketches. He played the straight man to my Uncle Fred's comic and my mother was the feed. He had a chance to settle down when the Empire Theatre was being built at Liverpool and Moss Empires offered him the job of chief scenic artist. But he preferred to be his own boss and so he designed and made the scenery for a sketch called 'Kurios' in which the family appeared. With 'Kurios' he was given a seven-year contract by Sir Oswald Stoll and began to make his name. He was the first man in British music hall to devise trick sets in which further, different sets developed, as if by magic, out of one.

This, then, was the family I was born into: a father who was a performer with a genius for scenery, a kindly, humorous man who, no matter what the provocation, never lifted a finger to my sister or myself; a hard-working mother devoted to my father. If there were any defects in their characters, I can't recall them. I was a happy child with loving parents. It was a good start.

There was no question about my future. In those days, if you were a butcher's boy, you became a butcher. If you were a doctor's son, you became a doctor. James Arthur Thomas Jewel Marsh Junior was destined for show business and at no time in my life did I ever think of anything else.

At first, though, I was happiest behind the scenes. My cousin, Ben Warriss, was the stage-struck member of the family. He was six months older than me and had been born in the same bed. Our mothers were sisters. Six months, when you are three or four, is a long time, and Ben was the boss, a dark kid with big ears. He had a beautiful voice and loved performing. Ben was a natural. We did our first double act when we were both about four, to a highly critical show-business audience of aunts and uncles in the drawing room in Cobden View Road. We rehearsed in the kitchen, watched by Chat, then made our entrance in our sailor suits singing:

The five fifteen, hear the whistle blowing.

I think we did all right. I don't know. But I remember a lot of kissing at the end. We were always kissing the aunts and uncles.

It was Ben who was to become the child performer, doing impressions of Nellie Wallace, while I was happier following my father around working on his sets. He used the drawing room as a scenic studio workshop and extended the garage to store the scenery. I watched him devise the trick sets and followed him around like a puppy, clutching a paint brush or a screwdriver in my small fist.

During the First World War he worked in Brown's steelyard and in the evening he gave charity shows at hospitals and works' canteens. Mona and my mother worked with him at these concerts and Cousin Ben did his impressions. I watched and listened. My father was beginning to develop a different act in which he played an idle husband and my mother was the nagging wife. I took mental notes, for this was my education, my real schooling. The other kind—of desks and blackboards—was a bit of a disaster.

From the beginning I hated it. My first school, was a bleak Victorian building in Broomhill. Ben and I went together. We lasted three days. We got up to so much mischief that the headmaster told our parents that he would take one of us but not both. A coin was tossed. Ben stayed and I went to another school for a while before it was decided that I should go to a boarding school called Burnetson College in Derbyshire.

It was an impressive enough looking place, an old country mansion with stables and playing fields. I hated it on sight. The headmaster, a cold man called Tearl, ushered my father away after the initial interview and I can still see him hurrying away in tears. He didn't say goodbye. All I saw was his bowler hat bobbing along by a hedge. I wasn't having it, and from the start I was a right little sod. I fought with everybody. There were two brothers called Abe and Cabe Baalam and I fought with them all the time. I wouldn't be bullied by them, or anyone.

Early one morning I went down to the stables where pigeons were kept in haylofts. I let all the pigeons out. I don't know whether they were the school's pets, but they certainly weren't homers. They all buggered off and never came back. Unsurprisingly I was called up in front of the headmaster and caned.

I lasted about a year. After one holiday break my father was set to take me back. We were having lunch in the County Hotel, Derby, and he met a man there who said he wasn't taking his son back to Burnetson because there was a lot of bullying going on. That was enough for my father. Instead of going back to the college we drove to the Palace Theatre, Leicester. I was the happiest eight-year-old in the north of England, no doubt about that.

The family were touring—playing a different town every week. I went to school wherever we were playing with the proviso that I was let out for matinées. I didn't learn much. It was a fairly eccentric method of education. Even now I can't add up (even with a calculator) nor can I spell too well. All my arithmetic was good for, later, was allowing me to know when I was being conned by an agent.

Childhood memories have little to do with schools. Teachers made very little impression upon me. The early days were a mish-mash of different towns, different landladies and different digs. I remember working on the paint frame at the Empire, Sheffield. My father was one of the first men to use aniline dye to paint his scenery and he had the pots lined up in front of the frame. I kicked over a green pot and it ran down the back wall of the stage where they had built a quick-change room for Sir Harry Lauder. His wigs were hanging on hooks and the aniline dye splashed onto one of them. I had given Harry Lauder green hair. But he was very good about it. He just laughed.

I remember, from that time, Dickie Henderson's father, Dickie Senior. He and my father were great friends and when they were on the same bill they liked to indulge in leg-pulling. There was an act that performed with them once at the Empire, Islington, called Mike Moritz and Acka. Like many of the animal acts in those days they weren't too fussy where they got their animals. They called their monkeys the Cuddly Chimps, but in fact they were monsters. The smallest was as big as Ronnie Corbett and they were a bit barmy. They were inverts, conceived incestuously by a male chimp and his daughter. They were cross-eyed and could be ferocious. In this particular act they cycled round the stage and did tricks behind a net which stretched around the stage. After they had

15

been pushed on, they couldn't get out, either towards the orchestra pit or into the wings. They just cycled around and did their tricks until they were led off. They were quite savage, some of them, bought cheaply from circuses and zoos because they had attacked people.

One night my father and Dickie Senior found two holes in the net at the back of the stage and stood there, hidden by the backcloth. As the chimps came round, first my father blew a raspberry and then Dickie Henderson followed suit.

The chimps glared at the net, looking for something to kill, but they didn't know what was going on. Eventually, on the third night, the biggest chimp figured it out. He cycled round towards where my father stood behind the backcloth.

'Brrrrp!' came the raspberry.

As the chimp passed the spot where my father was standing he threw himself off the bike and smashed him up against the back wall with a vicious backhander. The old man didn't blow any more raspberries after that!

These were the memories: touring with my parents, sharing a bed with Mona in digs that all seemed the same. The extraordinary affection I felt towards my family is probably rooted in the fact that I was hardly ever away from them. The towns changed, the digs changed, but the family was the constant factor, the centre of existence. I had no friends as a child, only Ben. Indeed, even at fifteen when my father bought me my first set of golf clubs in Norwich, I had no one my own age to play with and so I would go out and do eighteen holes on my own. Not that I ever felt deprived—I was a happy kid.

Three

When the First World War ended, my father was able to take his sketches on tour once more. He had devised a sketch called 'Idle-itis' about a nagging wife (played by my mother) who gets her doctor to prescribe pills to make her idle husband Simon Shirkit (played by my father) go to work. He takes the pills and starts seeing things. The room becomes haunted and the stage turns, first into Hell, then into the North Pole. Candles appear and disappear. Handkerchiefs fly from the poor man's hands and climb the wall. For a finale, the bed turns into a raging dragon.

I use the present tense to describe it because, although the set was blitzed during the Second World War, I was able to reconstruct it for pantomime and prove that his ideas worked long after his death.

'Idle-itis' opened at the Alhambra, Wombwell, in 1918 and ran for almost four years. It made his name, not only in the north but in London. He followed it with another sketch called 'A Daring Experiment' and then began to plan a full-length revue. But meanwhile we had an unexpected addition to the family.

My father had hired a prop boy called Johnny Foster. He was a little man from St. Helens, nice enough, a quiet sort. I vaguely remember Mona going away, leaving the show for a while; when she rejoined us she had a little baby with her and Johnny had become part of the family. I think my parents were upset because Johnny was just a prop boy and they probably had grander ideas for Mona. She was only sixteen when she and Johnny were married. It was all very hush-hush. Show-business families in those days had a rigid code. If a girl got pregnant, she and the man were made to marry. It didn't matter if they weren't in love. There was no choice. There was no moralising or anything. It was not considered disgraceful, just one of those things that happened, yet, at the same time, my parents did not want it known that Mona, at sixteen, was pregnant before she was married.

I went off shortly afterwards to a boarding school in Penge, in south London. It was run by two sisters and catered mainly for the children of show people. I stayed there for a year. I didn't mind it as much as Burnetson; but I didn't learn much either. All I wanted was to get back north and go on tour again.

By the time I got back, my father had bought a house in Salford, at 37 Howard Street. He paid eight hundred pounds for it and spent another three-hundred-and-fifty building a store in the back garden. It was a big building, to be used as a scene dock and to house a paint frame. We called it the stores, a hundred feet long by thirty-six feet wide and thirty feet high. As I watched the sections arriving by lorry, I realised how successful my father had become and almost before the roof was on I was in there with him working on the scenery for his new show.

For years he had been planning a revue. It was his ambition. He wanted to tour with his own show, so that he would not need to appear on other people's bills. He called his new show 'Explosions'. It was to open with a production scene followed by a sketch, another production scene, then a singer, a chorus, another sketch—eighteen scenes in all. The centre piece was a sketch in which a miner's parlour was transformed into a coal mine which caved in after an explosion and was then restored to the parlour. It was a complicated business involving a mere twenty-second blackout of the stage during which the scene was transformed, but it proved to be a success and enhanced his reputation.

'Explosions' took two years to plan and build. He hired a scriptwriter called Con West to knock out material including the lyrics, and slowly the revue began to take shape. I worked on the scenery and backcloths, great sheets of canvas, thirty to forty feet wide and thirty feet deep. These cloths, when painted, helped to distinguish our company from the others. People who remember only the last knockings of variety can have no idea of the glamour of a James A. Jewel show. The playwright Alan Ayckbourn tells a story of two women who had been coaxed into a theatre at Scarborough after years of watching black-and-white television. As they walked in and saw the set, one turned to the other and said approvingly: 'Oh, look. It's in colour.' That was one of the attractions: the colour, and I'm sure we added a splash to people's lives.

As we built up towards the opening of the show, my father and I worked non-stop in the stores, sleeping in armchairs. My mother brought in the meals which she cooked between working with Mona on the costumes. Johnny was the 'gofer', going out for the materials: the canvas, wood, screws, glue, cloth and binding and the glitter.

'Explosions' opened at the Hippodrome, Mexborough, in the summer of 1925. The company consisted of the family and cousin Ben plus Walter and Elsie Vedale who did a musical act, a juvenile lead called Jach Sheridan (son of the great comic Mark Sheridan), a feed called Freddy Read; Jack Fentiman was the conductor; there were eight chorus girls hired from a dancing school in Middlesborough, and the backstage staff.

I had a walk-on part playing a telegraph boy in one of the sketches. Ben had a little song and the part of the miner's boy saved by my father in the main scene when the pit roof caved in.

After a few weeks, my father realised that the show was top-heavy. There were too many people. The box office returns couldn't maintain such a large company and reluctantly he decided to prune it. He couldn't sack me because I wasn't getting paid, but Ben was—and so he had to go. When Ben's father heard the news, he went crazy. He was a dark little man with a bit of a temper.

On the Saturday night when the show finished, he arrived at the theatre—the Grand, Doncaster—and created hell. There was a fight backstage. For some reason he hit Johnny Foster. My father got him by the arms and pushed him against a flat. As I watched all this, Ben crept up behind me,

19

clouted me on the side of the face, ran upstairs to a dressing room and locked himself in. I couldn't get at him.

The two sides of the family didn't speak for years after that. In fact, when 'Explosions' played Sheffield, we heard that Ben's father had threatened to have us done over; but nothing happened. It wasn't until long afterwards when my niece Betty fell ill that we were reconciled.

With Ben gone, I got the part of the miner's boy. As my father sang: 'Blue Bells Are Gathered', I came on with his tea. The roof caved in but he saved me. As I lay trapped, he pleaded:

'Don't worry about me. Take care of the kid. . . .

There was another twenty-second blackout and my mother was discovered asleep in her armchair in front of the fire. Two men came in carrying a stretcher covered with a blanket. My mother knelt by the stretcher and said: 'Come on. Speak to me Simon. Tell me you're not hurt.' My father sat up. He was wearing a paper hat.

'I've been to a party,' he said.

The pit explosion had been my mother's dream.

That was my introduction to performing but it wasn't long before I got my first speaking role. Jack Sheridan left the show and my father decided to give me his part in a sketch called 'Tripe Supper'. I was to play a half-wit, trying to chat up a girl played by Mona.

'Act daft,' said my father at rehearsals.

'Okay,' I said. I thought about it and decided to do it with a stutter. It seemed to work in rehearsal and my father agreed. He also put me on the bill for the first time—as Marsh Jewel.

I went on at some No. 3 theatre and stammered out my lines. The audience laughed and I liked their reaction. I think I made up my mind there and then that I wanted to be a performer. Until then I had been quite content to stage-manage and work behind the scenes, but I liked the sound of laughter. It wasn't a great Road-to-Damascus discovery. No bolts of lightning shook the stage. I didn't come off and scream to the rafters that a new comic star was born. I just said to my father: 'This is what I'd like to do.'

He nodded. 'Well, if that's it, then you've got to learn the whole business.'

There were no hysterics, no tears of happiness that I was following in his footsteps. It had always been assumed that, sooner or later, I would do it. Just a nod from him and a smile. But I'm sure he was delighted and he began to look around for people to teach me.

The first was Henry Vale who, as part of an act called the Four Wards, had worked with my father in a show called 'Dancing Time'. Henry had just come back from Canada and was looking for a job. My father said he could come as assistant stage manager if he taught me to dance.

I had met him as a child and liked him. He was a character, a big man, in his late twenties, a six-footer with a broken nose, a wild man from Islington—which in those days was a hard part of London. He could get everything he owned into a brown-paper parcel which he called his cabin trunk and he could fart every note of 'Bye Bye Blackbird'.

Every morning for four months he taught me to dance. He taught me Lancashire clog dancing and soft-shoe, what we called close-to-the-floor dancing. He taught me tap dancing, to buck and wing. And we danced together in the show—a shadow dance where I played a jewel thief and he played a police sergeant chasing me. For Henry the role of policeman was the exact opposite of his nature and I think he took a perverse delight in putting on the uniform.

After that, I began to learn to tumble. My father had brought in a circus act called the Stebbing Brothers and in the mornings I watched them practise. One day I asked them to show me, and they strapped me into a leather belt with ropes attached called a lunge. I practised back somersaults with the Stebbings holding on to the ropes so that I wouldn't land on my head. I learned upstarts, flip-flaps and somersaults and it took me six months before I was ready to go on with them. At sixteen, a lot of the suppleness has gone. To be a proper acrobat, you have to start young.

Eventually the Stebbings and my father decided I was ready. We called ourselves the Three Imps and we opened the act at the Opera House, Wakefield.

For our act the old man painted a surround of Hell with a fan at the back of the stage and silks fluttering like flames. He had some kind of fascination for Hell and devils and ghosts. He could never pass a ghost train at a fun fair without studying it. Once he painted a picture of his idea of Hades. It was strange, like a Salvador Dali painting.

As one of the Imps I was dressed once more in a leotard and horns—full-sized horns this time. We did the act, tumbling, rolling, flipping and somersaulting just as we had rehearsed. The finishing trick was the 'Three Man High', in which we stood on one another's shoulders then collapsed slowly, did a roll-over, then got up and bowed to the audience. That was the theory. I, being the lightest, was the top man. We stood on one side of the stage; there was a drum roll and down I went. What I didn't know was that one of the trap doors was old and rotten. I hit it and went straight through into a cess-pit. I clambered out and faced the audience covered in shit.

It was the curse of the red leotard again. Bloody leotards. Bloody horns.

'Explosions' ran for three years and my father played it for all it was worth, taking it twice round the theatre circuit. It was almost impossible to run out of theatres in those days. There were fifteen variety theatres in the Manchester area alone and the same number around Liverpool. We travelled as far as Glasgow and Exeter and toured the No. 2 theatres in London.

We did two shows a night, ringing up at six-thirty, down at eight-thirty, up again fifteen minutes later and down at ten-thirty or eleven. We did this six nights a week with two matinées. On the Saturday night we packed our traps and loaded the cloths and scenery onto two fourteen-foot horse-drawn lorries and drove them to the station where we had to load everything into a twenty-one-foot railway truck. My father wouldn't hire a thirty-footer, which would have been easier, because there was a deal with the railways that gave ten free tickets with the hire of the shorter one. Once it was loaded, we went to the next town and went through the same operation in reverse. I was lucky if I got to bed on a Sunday morning before four. On the Monday I was up at six to go to the station and unload the railway truck onto the horsedrawn wagons so that the stuff would be in the theatre by eight-thirty.

It was non-stop action and we played some strange theatres. The Palace Theatre, Bradford, was built underneath the Princess Theatre, which did only straight plays. If our orchestra played too loudly, the 'legitimate' audience upstairs could hear it, and when we did the coal mine scene with the explosions, they must have thought another war had started.

The Broadhead Tour round Manchester was also a bit odd because old man Percy Broadhead would not pay the Electricity Board prices. He installed his own generators but they were forever breaking down and it was not unusual to find yourself in the middle of a scene when suddenly everything went black.

The living was often hard and income sometimes barely met expenditure. The company had grown with the addition of Henry Vale and the Stebbings, plus the occasional unexpected extra.

We were playing the Hippodrome, Mexborough when my parents were told that Jack Fentiman's wife wanted to see them. Jack was the conductor and his wife toured with us.

'Come in,' said my father.

And a complete stranger walked in.

'I am the real Mrs Fentiman,' she announced. 'That other woman is his fancy piece, Maisie Howard. I want you to sack him.' My father shook his head. He wouldn't sack Jack and the result was that the three of them lived together. Jack slept with both of them.

Later the real wife became pregnant but the child died. And later still she was crippled and Maisie pushed her around in a wheelchair.

We called Jack The Man With The Load Of Mischief.

Now, of course, the Depression was beginning to bite and often the takings amounted to less than the one-hundred-and-twenty pounds which was needed to keep the company afloat. What held the system together was the enthusiasm of the performers and the loyalty of the audiences for whom the show was the only piece of good news. We played some bleak and desolate places where the streets were filled with smoke and rain and the people had had the stuffing knocked out of them by low wages—or by no wages at all.

Yet somehow we managed to live with some style. A tailor called Joe Bloom in Birmingham made all our clothes and he wasn't in a hurry for his bills. We paid him when we could and occasionally, when we were playing If-it shows, it was later rather than sooner. If-it shows were quite common—if the money came in, you got it; if it didn't, you got nothing. But a suit was only six pounds and digs were cheap. Fifty bob bought a couple of bedrooms and a sitting room and the star of the show always got the best digs. My father had the pickings of the digs and normally we were quite comfortable. I shared a bed for years with Henry Vale, which wasn't too bad except for Saturday nights when he was drunk and it would be an odorous solo of 'Bye Bye Blackbird'. The landladies did the catering. My mother would write ahead saying what time we would arrive on a Sunday and gave her order for roast lamb, Yorkshire and two veg.

And no matter how tight things were, we had to have a car. Many of my early memories are to do with cars. They were necessities. I learned to drive my father's Morris Oxford when I was fourteen and it was not long before I was in trouble. We were playing the Theatre Royal, Rawtenstall, and on the Sunday we arrived, I went to the local pub where my parents were having their customary Sunday drink with members of the company.

'Can I put the car in the garage Dad? Please Dad, eh?'

The garage was just around the corner.

'Go on then,' he said.

So I drove off round the corner, full of good intentions but lacking a licence. I thought I might as well take one tour round the block. As I came round the corner I saw Fred Read, our juvenile lead with Ted Drew, the assistant stage manage, and two chorus girls.

'My father's lent me the car,' I said. 'How about a spin in the country?'

The spin lasted as far as the first T-junction where I bumped a motor-cycle sidecar. Fred Read quickly changed places with me and gave the motor cyclist my father's name and a false address.

Six months later Dad and I were in the stores and my mother came in saying that someone from the insurance company was enquiring about a road accident. The motor cyclist and my father were insured by the same company and they were checking all the Marshes on their books. My father said he did not know anything about it and we heard no more. It was years before I owned up and told him what had happened.

Even without a licence, though, I was a better driver than my father. He was hopeless. I was guiding him into our garage one morning, with my back to the wall and he drove right up me so that the mudguard was aimed between my legs.

'Stop,' I said.

He stopped.

'Reverse,' I said.

He pushed at the gear stick, let out the clutch and the car moved *forward*, pinning me to the wall like a butterfly.

'Reverse,' I squealed but he was so scared that he jumped out of the car and ran to the house for help, came back with a couple of friends and together they manhandled the car off me. There were a lot of bad jokes made after that about my marriage prospects. As well as being a bit dodgy with gearsticks he had no sense of direction. I had to meet him one day in Thames Ditton. I saw him coming from a long way off in the Sunbeam, jumped into a friend's car and drove to the turning to meet him. I assumed that he would go past the turning because he could never home in on anything, but this time he turned straight in and we crashed.

There were two coppers on the corner, a young one and a sergeant. The sergeant said to his colleague: 'Go and get the young feller's licence. I'll get the other one.'

'Right.'

They took down our particulars and met again in the middle of the road.

'Well?' said the sergeant.

'He's James Arthur Thomas Marsh, 37 Howard Street Salford.'

'No, that can't be right.'

'Well, it is.'

'You bloody idiot, you've got the same licence as I have: James Arthur Thomas Marsh, 37 Howard Street, Salford.'

'I can't have.'

25

'There can't be two blokes with the same driving licence, you fool.'

The sergeant came across to my father.

'What's your name?'

'James Arthur Thomas Marsh, 37 Howard Street Salford.'

'There you are,' he said to the young one. 'Told you didn't I?'

Then to me.

'What's your name?'

'James Arthur Thomas. . . .'

'Oh, Christ!'

We sorted it out eventually.

Whenever we were together, I usually drove. One Christmas we went from Manchester to Sheffield to see my niece Betty, who had been in hospital for some time. Each year my father made something for the children in the ward; a toy or a piece of scenery. This particular year he had made a six-foot high windmill with three-foot sails. We strapped it on to the roof of Mona's old Morris, which she had bought for three pounds from a scrap dealer.

The weather was bad and the route took us through the notorious Snake Head Pass over the Pennines. It was always one of the first roads to get blocked in winter and most years someone plunged over into the valley. We made it to Sheffield, delivered the windmill, spent a few hours with Betty and started back.

It grew dark. I switched on the lights but the only one working was the offside side-lamp. I looked at my father. He shrugged and gazed through the windscreen.

'Drive on, young Jim.'

He probably thought it was nothing. After all, he was an old hand at the Snake Head Pass. I peered through the windscreen and drove as much by instinct as by vision, but I thought I could make it all right, so long as the motor stayed in one piece. Half an hour into the Pass, the bloody thing slewed to one side. I stopped the car and we got out. One of the front tyres had blown. We cursed and shivered. It was pitch dark now and below freezing. We searched for the jack but there was no jack; what's more there was no spare wheel; but in such circumstances, you are forced to use some imagination. There were some short pieces of wood under one of the cushions and a handy rock by the verge. Using the rock as a fulcrum, we managed to lift the axle and get the wheel off. I took out the inner tube and we stuffed the tyre case with grass and put it back on.

We prayed a bit I think, and the old man sang to keep our spirits up. I could hardly steer the motor; then, even as we were congratulating ourselves on our enterprise, one of the back wheels blew and we almost pitched over into the valley.

We climbed out again, searching for another rock and more grass. The same operation. Slowly the little car made its way deeper into the Pennines, higher and higher. We were crawling home, fingers and toes crossed. Then, just as we reached a slope, the steering went altogether. I thought it was a third tyre but when I looked down, the wheel had come off in my hand. The locking nut had worked its way clear. I hit the brakes and the old car lurched to a stop. Below us in the pitch darkness was a drop of God knows how many feet—enough to kill us, anyway. If we'd had four good tyres, we would have gone over the edge for sure. It was only the grass in the tyre cases that had slowed us sufficiently to allow me to make an emergency stop.

I looked at my old man. His face resembled an unset jelly but I could tell he was fighting to remain calm—nonchalant even, the man in charge.

'By 'eck lad,' he croaked. 'Are we going to get there for closing time or not?'

It was a brave effort and I laughed. Closing time indeed. It might have been closing time for good for the Jewels.

I reversed back from the edge, screwed the steering wheel back on and slowly we headed for home.

It took us five hours to make a journey that normally took an hour and a quarter, yet we walked into the house in triumph. A white hare had wandered into the road; it probably didn't see the car, with only the one tiny light blinking. I hit it fair and square. And so we walked into the house, holding it by the ears.

'Jugged hare for Christmas,' said the old man happily, looking for all the world like the great white hunter.

Four

Show-business routine tended to follow a fairly predictable pattern for some—

Morning: down to the theatre to pick up any mail. Buy a newspaper and wander round the town.

Lunchtime: the local pub, meet the other pros; gossip, swap anecdotes, grumble about business.

Afternoon: at throwing-out time, wander back to the digs, take a nap.

Evening: work.

It was hardly a glamorous life. There were long periods of hanging around which suited some people, but not my father. He was not a pub man. He found it difficult to relax, a trait which I have inherited from him. Our practice was to be in the theatre by ten to rehearse new sketches, songs and dance numbers. If a new sketch was planned, then scenery had to be made. After lunch we were back in the theatre with the glue pot on the gas ring and the hammers and saws in our hands.

Whenever there was any time off, he would be thinking of the next show. In the three years while 'Explosions' ran, he made plans for his next revue, to be called 'Pop Inn'. Whenever he had time out, he got out the workshop tools and began to make new scenery. I helped him and I was never happier than when I was working alongside him with the scenery. It was from him that I inherited the itch to work. The only time I was away from it was on the golf course. When the others were in the pubs and when there was no work to do, I would find the local course and play eighteen holes. I didn't drink or smoke then; I fancied myself as a bit of an athlete.

Sundays was 'boxing day'. In the morning I went down to Harry Fleming's gym in the Oldham Road, Manchester and in the afternoons I went with my father to see the fights at the Ardwick Stadium. Fleming's gym was a typical sweat-box above a row of shops. At first I just watched and worked out on the punch bags and the speed bags. I had my own gloves—and a punchball back at the stores—and I was quite fast with a good right. There were a number of fine fighters there: Jacky Brown the flyweight, Jock McEvoy and Johnny King, the British bantamweight champion.

Eventually I went into the ring and sparred. I worked out for about a year there and began to think that perhaps I could make it as a professional. Then one afternoon I went in with Len Johnson, who I think would have been British light-heavyweight champion if they had allowed blacks to fight for the title. Len whacked me all around the ring for three rounds. I turned it in after that. I climbed out of the ring, picked up my gloves, left, and never went back.

Nonetheless, Fleming's gym came in handy because show business could be rough in those days.

In Ashington, for example, we had a bit of bother with a stage manager and a drop roller—which was an advert-sheet on a two-foot cylinder which dropped in front of us in place of a curtain.

I'd already had a bit of an argument with this feller. Big bloke he was, a miner. All the stage hands we hired there were miners. They'd come straight up from the pit with coal dust on their faces.

On the first night, at the end of the first show we were all lined up taking a bow when the stage manager let the drop roller down and it missed us by a fraction. My father walked off.

'Listen,' he said. 'Next time, let us take a step back before you drop the roller.' The stage manager said nothing.

We were taking the bow at the end of the second house when down came the roller again, hit Walter Vedale on the bugle and made it bleed. My father stormed off.

'If that happens tomorrow,' he said. 'I will personally come off the stage and hit you over the head with a bracecrash.'

It was no idle threat. A bracecrash is a collection of metal bars tied together which is used to make off-stage noises. When it is dropped, the audience thinks the house has come down. A bracecrash in the hands of an angry man like my father would do a lot of damage.

The stage manager didn't say a word. He just took a swing at the old man. My father went underneath it, swung him round, hit him on the chin and knocked him clear into the orchestra pit. Next, all the men in the show cleared off, leaving me and the old man to face seven stage hands. There we were with our backs to the roller, chopping them down as they came at us; at the other side the audience was filing out, not knowing anything was going on.

My mother looked out from one of the dressing rooms, saw what was happening and let Peter the dog out. I can still hear her.

'Go get them, Peter.'

He was an Alsatian. In two seconds he had cleared the stage. He stood there wagging his tail, chewing the bits of britches in his mouth. But we had to have police protection after that. We carried hammers with us all week...

In Bargoed, South Wales, though, I didn't have a hammer, but I could have used one. One big miner stage hand had been a nuisance all week. Like some of his mates he thought he could take the micky out of us. Show business folk were pansies—that was his idea. On the Saturday night he was drunk and he wasn't being too careful with the scenery. It was fragile and easily broken. I saw him pick up a piece which we called the Cleopatra couch and throw it across the stage towards the dock doors where we were loading. It smashed; so I had a go at him. He just grinned; then I whacked him. He was so big I had to jump in the air to hit him but I knew I'd hit him right. He should have gone, but he didn't. He just stood there and laughed at me—and that must be the most frightening thing in the world, because you know you've got no chance. He picked me up in a bear hug.

'Oh Christ,' I said.

I saw my father coming behind him. He tried to pull the big man off me but couldn't, so he hit him over the back of the head with an iron brace. It made no difference. The guy just

30

kept smiling and we both knew at that instant that were in for it. He did the pair of us in style and not even Peter would have helped. He'd have probably eaten Peter.

We were always dodging trouble in Wales. I remember an old man watching us fitting up at a theatre in Tonypandy. My father was grumbling about the facilities. The flash boxes didn't work properly. He had a Lyon's treacle tin which he had converted into a kind of flashgun using powder called Licapodium. This stuff came from Russia; it was a kind of pollen, very expensive, and when it was lit there was a terrific flash; but something was going wrong with it that morning and my father kept on moaning.

The old man watched in silence. He had a wooden leg which he rested on the orchestra rail.

Eventually everything was fitted up and that night the show went well. When it was over, the old man turned up backstage and announced that he was the owner of the theatre.

'You were doing a lot of complaining,' he said to my father.
'Yes, well. . . .'
'It was lucky for you, boyo, the show was a success,' he said gravely, 'because if it had flopped, I'd have belted you with this.' And he tapped his wooden leg.

He would have too. . . .

But although stage hands and owners could be a problem, you knew where you stood with them. They weren't half as bad as some people who hung around wanting to buy drinks all the time. There was one feller in Bradford, a bookie who was also a town councillor. He kept coming round after the show and asking my father to have a drink with him. The old man put him off, politely. He wasn't much of a drinker and at the end of the night all he wanted was to go back to the digs, get the beans and the pies out and sit by the fire.

One Thursday, the councillor became insistent. He followed us up the stairs from the dressing room and out into the street.

'Come for a drink,' he said. 'You and your wife.'
'Thanks for the offer,' said the old man, 'but we've done three shows today; we're dead beat.'
'So tha'll not come for a drink then?'
'No.'

31

'Then tha's a ***.'

There was a taxi waiting for the councillor with both its passenger doors open. The old man hit him so hard he knocked him through the taxi and out the other side on to the road. He had a police whistle, this bloke, and as he lay there he started blowing it.

'Come on,' I said, bundled my father and mother into our car and drove to the digs.

Next morning I went to the theatre to collect the mail, then to a gunsmith's to pick up the big .45 revolver we used as a prop. It was a huge thing and fired blanks; the gunsmith had been fitting it with a new firing-pin. After that I went back to our digs.

When I got there, two town councillors were talking to my father. Our man from the night before had lost two teeth and he was waiting for some sort of recompense at the Queen's Hotel.

'If you don't apologise, he'll cause trouble,' one of the councillors said. My father was all for leaving it, but I persuaded him to go and sort the problem out. We drove down there. It was about twelve: High Noon.

He was waiting for us in one of the bedrooms. He pointed to the gap where his teeth used to be and demanded an apology.

My father shook his head. 'I don't let anybody use bad language in front of my wife,' he said.

'Then tha'll not apologise?'

'Correct.'

He led us over and pointed through the window. Two men stood at the corner. 'If tha doesn't apologise ...' he said, 'they'll have thee.' And did a little mime, of a razor being drawn across my father's face. That got me. I wasn't having it. I reached into my coat and pulled out the .45.

'If you touch him,' I said, 'I'll blow your bloody head off.'

He went white and I learned something there and then. If you point a revolver at someone he doesn't look to see whether or not the barrel is blocked off.

'Oh Christ,' he said.

Just then and with perfect timing, there was a knock on the door.

As I shoved the gun into my pocket, the Chief Constable

walked in. We knew him. His name was Porter. One of the councillors must have told him what was going on. He looked at our man.

'We've had a lot of trouble with you,' he said. 'Leave Mister Jewel alone.'

The councillor pointed at me.

'He threatened me with a soddin' gun.'

'Who? Me?' I looked as innocent as I was able.

That was Bradford. *We* got out of it in one piece.

When 'Explosions' finished, we went back to Salford to prepare for 'Pop Inn'. For eight weeks, my father and I worked non-stop in the stores. One of my jobs was to hang the back cloths on the paint frame, stretching them across the frame prior to painting them. The normal way to do this was to climb ladders and proceed inch by inch but I discovered that it was quicker to clamber on to the top stay and straddle it like a sailor, pulling the cloth behind me. It worked well until one afternoon when I reached the stay and it tore away, swinging me thirty-four feet to the floor. I landed on my toes.

'Are you all right?' my father asked.

Before I could answer, his eyes rolled back and he fainted. I had to get a brandy to revive him. When he came to, he said that he had never seen such a stunt. But for me, it was par for the course. All my life I've fallen off things or crashed into things.

In those eight weeks we grabbed meals and ate on our feet, snatching a few hours sleep in armchairs. When we had finished, we came out into the garden, blinking in the sunlight like a pair of moles. My father squinted at me.

'You look like Jesus Christ,' he said.

I did. I'd grown a beard in there; but it soon came off because I had decided that I wanted to become a juvenile lead—the suave young entertainer who does the song and dance stuff, dressed in top hat, muffler and overcoat. I had had a hankering to do this sort of work ever since the first days of 'Explosions'. I had seen Jack Buchanan at the opening night of 'One Damn Thing After Another' at the Palace Theatre, Manchester. My father had taken me as a treat and after the show we had dinner at the Midland Hotel. The restaurant was packed with theatre-goers and at midnight Buchanan walked in with some of the cast. Everyone stood up and applauded. It was wonderful and I thought: 'This is for me.' I reckoned I'd be good at it. I did impressions of Chevalier and I fancied myself as a bit of a singer and dancer.

The ambition was strengthend at the Old Hippodrome, Dudley, when I met a man called Billy Childs. I was working on a paint frame when he walked in, and the man impressed me immediately. He was in his early thirties, a tall fair-haired cockney wearing a sharp suit. He was a charmer, a song and dance man. My father decided to hire him for 'Pop Inn' to give the show, he said, a touch of class.

Late when we played London, I watched Billy drive off with his Mayfair friends to the West End night clubs. I was green with envy. He was friendly with a Lord at that time and to me, at seventeen, that was quite something. Billy taught me to tootle on alto sax and we did a duet of 'Moonlight and Roses' which often sounded like Henry doing his 'Blackbird'. Meanwhile I practised being suave.

And one night at the Opera House, Wakefield, I went on as a juvenile lead for the first time singing 'Here I Am, Broken-hearted'. But even then, in my top hat and muffler, I could still get myself into trouble.

I followed a sketch with my song. The sketch involved pots and pans being thrown around. When it finished, I came on, in front of the curtain and calmed down the audience with 'Here I am Broken-hearted'. In the middle I had a short *recitative*. The audience listened politely and silently as I went into it:

That was the tale he related
My heart went out to him there.
He said: I guess it was fated,
They'd have made a wonderful pair.

It was lump-in-the-throat material but right in the middle of my speech, the prop boy behind the curtain emptied one bucket of pots into another. There was an almighty crash. I opened the tabs, kicked him up the backside for his clumsiness, turned back to the audience, finished the song, bowed and went off.

He was waiting for me in the wings and met me with a

34

right-hander, straight in the mouth. I went back to take a call, came off and walked into another right-hander. I couldn't get off. I came back, bowed, off again and *bang*, he hit me again. I kept taking curtain calls but the next production scene had begun and no-one was applauding me. By this time my nose was bleeding and so, next time, I ducked under the punch and hit him. My father rushed at us.

'If you want to fight,' he said. 'Do it after the show.'

'Right,' I said.

As soon as the final curtain came down, I had my tailcoat off and I was at him, ready to get stuck in. He was about the same age as me, the same weight but he didn't want to know.

'Wait a minute,' he said as I squared up to him. 'Nine o'clock in t' morning and bring thee clogs.'

I said: 'Pardon?'

'Nine o'clock and bring thee clogs.'

I let him go and wandered across the road to the pub where we were staying. The landlord was washing glasses and I told him what the boy had said.

'Don't stand for that, Jim,' he said. 'They chalk a circle on the ground. You stand inside it, the both of you, with your clogs, and kick each other. We call it purrin' in Yorkshire.'

I didn't fancy that. Next morning I turned up. Sure enough, there he was with his clogs and a piece of chalk.

'I'm not having that,' I said.

'Well, I'm not having that,' he said, pointing to my fists. So we agreed to call it off.

About two weeks later we were playing the Hippodrome, Mexborough, and I saw a group of miners come out of a pub. Two of them put their clogs on, climbed into a barrel and began kicking each other. This lasted a few minutes before one of them came out with no cobblers.

They were strange people. You were never sure what they would do next. They had odd habits. One week we were playing Alfreton near Derby and again we were staying in a pub. A feller came in one lunchtime, carrying a sack. It was moving.

My father looked at the barman. 'What's he got in there?'

'Rats,' said the barman. 'He's the rat-catcher.'

The rat-catcher grinned at us.

'He'll do a trick for you if you want,' said the barman.

'Oh yeah?' said my father. 'What's that?'

'If you buy him a pint, he'll bite one of their heads off.'

We looked at one another and back at the rat-catcher. He was still grinning and nodding in agreement. The sack twitched. My father put his hand in his pocket and tossed a coin onto the counter.

'Have a pint then,' he said.

The rat-catcher took a gulp from the glass, reached into the sack, pulled out a live rat, bit its head off, spat it out, threw the body back into the sack and reached for his pint again.

That was enough for the old man and me. He didn't finish his beer that morning.

Meanwhile the company continued to grow. Billy Reilly, the Gallant Hussar, joined us. He played concertina and wore a hussar's uniform while he squeezed out military tunes. He was a big man, stocky and fair-haired with a boyish face.

One day I caught my father looking at Billy, Henry Vale and myself. He was thinking. I could tell. Billy had been a wrestler, Henry had fought quite a bit on the cobbles in Islington. I had done my share in Fleming's gym. Maybe he could capitalise on this for Friday night, traditionally the worse night of the week. People did their shopping on Friday nights. They didn't go to the theatre.

He had tried to lure them in with a greasy pole stunt. He would fix an old telegraph pole on trestles on stage, put me, Henry or Billy on the pole with a pillow and invite Friday nighters to have a go at us.

'Knock him off and win ten bob,' he said.

And they did. He gave away more ten bobs than Soft Mick. But maybe boxing. . . ?

So we built a ring and hauled it on stage on a Friday night. Then Henry, Billy and I paraded in front of the cloth in our vests and shorts and boxing gloves; me at ten-and-a-half stone, Henry at twelve, Billy at thirteen. We stood there like the three wise monkeys looking out into an audience of miners.

'Three pounds for anyone who can last three rounds with one of my fighters,' yelled my old man, like some fairground

36

booth promoter. Of course they queued up to have a go at us. The tickets were only one and sixpence and three pounds was a fortune. Bloody great miners.

Henry was okay, but Billy and I usually got a whacking. If we were getting too badly hurt, my father would jump in and shout 'foul' which usually got the audience angry. There were more fights in the stalls than there were on stage.

My father gave away handfuls of pound notes. It didn't last long, that idea, and I can't say I was sorry when we finally dismantled the ring. For a suave juvenile lead, going on with a black eye was not quite the right image.

Still, I was enjoying myself. The role of juvenile lead had its perks. I was quite good-looking in those days. I still had my hair and I didn't look too bad in my coat and muffler.

The word 'groupie' didn't exist then, but the girls were real enough. They queued at the stage door. I would give one of them the wink from the stage and as often as not, she would be waiting after the show. But there was a standard code of conduct. I realised early on that it was better to stick with the girls in the audience than to mess around with those in the business.

When I was fifteen I had fallen in love with a chorus girl called Gloria Douthwaite. She was eighteen. I remember that when she left the show at Ipswich one of my father's songs, in our show, was 'All Alone by the Telephone'. I was miserable for a while; but I never really mixed business with pleasure. The old man drummed it into me not to foul the nest. The girls at the stage door were all right, though.

I'd borrow the car saying I was going to play cards. In fact, I'd be at the Manchester Ritz with a girl. When I came back at one or two in the morning my father would stick his head out of the window and yell: 'You been playing cards again, you bloody liar?'

Each Sunday night, once we had got to a new town and unloaded, Henry Vale and I would take the car and go looking for birds. More often than not we found them. It was easy for Henry because he liked all women; in other words, he wasn't fussy. He picked up a girl in a bar in Hull one evening and looked at me inquiringly.

'No no,' I said. 'You go ahead.'

37

She was on the game, and a bit drunk.

I heard him negotiating with her.

'How much for the night, luv?'

'Thirty bob.'

'Okay.' He fished in his pocket. 'If I give you a pound and you give me ten bob, then we're right, eh?'

Next morning I was unloading the scenery from the railway truck when Henry turned up with a smile on his face and a pocket full of necklaces and silver frames he'd nicked from her room. He'd no scruples, Henry.

I remember a Luton barmaid I met when I was about sixteen. She took me down an alley, told me that she couldn't have children and that I could do whatever I liked. It was great; we were down the alley every night. One afternoon I thought I'd surprise her by turning up at her house. She had about eight kids. It frightened the life out of me.

Then there was the Castleford landlady. I was booked into the Queen's Theatre, Castleford, and Bert Tyas, the stage manager, met me at the station. Bert loved my family and I'd known him since I was a boy. I'd written ahead asking if he could find me digs and, as we were walking along the platform, he gave me the address.

'Twenty-five bob all in,' he said. 'And you'll be all right there, young Jim. She tekks t'watter.'

'Pardon?'

'The landlady. She tekks t'watter.'

'What do you mean, she takes water?'

'She fooks,' he said.

And she did. She was about three times my age, wasn't very beautiful and left nudist magazines lying round as a hint. I had a good time in Castleford.

I was about eighteen when I had my first really serious love affair. I was at home in Salford working on scenery when I got a telegram telling me to go to the Hippodrome, Salford. They needed a juvenile lead. I met a man called Tom Moss there who told me the story. He had had a juvenile lead called Pat Lennox who did an impression of Chevalier. There was also a girl in the show called Kathleen Ellis: blonde, very sexy, very knowledgeable and quite a few years older than me. She had been having an affair with Lennox. When the show played Carlisle, Moss had persuaded them to go off to Gretna Green and get married. So they did—and got publicity for the show. But when they got to Salford, Lennox disappeared with a girl called Vera, the other half of his double act, leaving Tom without a juvenile lead and Kathleen with a broken heart.

So I arrived in the scene and took over from Lennox. First stop was the Pavilion, Liverpool. We were all in the same digs, Tom Moss, his brother Joe and his girl friend, and Kathleen Ellis. I started to chat her up and we ended up living together, first in Liverpool, then on the Isle of Man during the summer season.

Halfway through the season, my father and mother came over to see us. They were very much against the liason. They didn't like Kathleen much. She was the Older Woman, with a bit of a reputation; but I was in love for the first time.

There had been a lot of birds and a lot of good times but I suppose, like any young man, I knew that one day I would meet someone who was important, someone I couldn't just walk away from. I had all kinds of plans for Kathleen Ellis.

When the season ended, she got a job with a guy called Joey Porter and went off on tour with him. I went back to Salford and sulked. After a few days I heard that she was having it off with Joey Porter. I was very young and very impressionable. I went down to the Trafford Arms and got drunk on port. It was the first time I had had a drink. I'd been in pubs but I always took ginger beer. I got drunk, on my own, from about seven till ten and I thought: 'I'll kill her.'

I went home, got out the .45 revolver and stumbled off to the station. I thought I'd frighten her to death with the bloody thing. I remember getting to Piccadilly Station, Manchester, buying a ticket for London and sitting in the train at midnight with the revolver, waiting to go. Kathleen and Joey were playing the Queen's Theatre, Poplar. I reckoned I'd get there during the night and surprise them but just as the train was about to pull out my father roared up in his car, jumped out and dragged me off the train and called me a silly sod. I don't know how he knew where I was. Henry Vale must have seen me at the house and added two and two. Henry, of course, would have let me go, just for the laugh. But not my father. He took me home and that was that. Even so, it took me a long time to get over Kathleen Ellis.

It was almost fifty years before I touched alcohol again. I've never tasted beer in my life. One lunchtime in Salford I was walking past the Cattle Market Hotel and a man came out and spewed brown ale in front of me. It put me off beer for life.

I had also seen how drink could finish people. I saw what it did to a lot of people in the business. There was a great comic called Claud Lester who was a brilliant comedian but with a weakness for booze. When Lester was playing the Holborn Empire, Val Parnell gave instructions that he should be locked in his dressing room after the first act because he was regularly drunk during his spot in the second act. One night he had managed to get something to drink and came on more than a little the worse for wear. He had smuggled a ball of string into the dressing room, thrown down some money to a boy in the street and, asked the kid to buy him a bottle. He was lucky that he found an honest kid who did what he asked. Claud pulled the bottle up on the string and got stuck into it.

At the Empire, Gateshead, once he grabbed a knife and chased an agent called Hymie Zhal through the pass door and right round the theatre backstage yelling for Hymie to give him a sub on his wages so that he could buy booze. Unsurprisingly, it finally killed him.

I swore it would never happen to me. I had great will power in those days. I haven't any will power now, otherwise I'd give up smoking. My father was the same about liquor. I saw him drunk only once in his life. I went to collect him from the Prince's Theatre, Accrington, and there he was, drinking with the stage manager. There were two empty whisky bottles on the table. I hauled him home and put him to bed; the next day he must have been feeling pretty ill because he couldn't even drive his car. I had to drive for him, which was a bit dodgy as I had a broken arm at the time.

The next time (after the Kathleen Ellis affair) that I had a drink was at the Nottingham Playhouse in 1975. I had been playing a dramatic scene in 'Comedians' and my legs kept stiffening up. One night the director, Richard Eyre, came backstage and said: 'You seemed to be swaying about out there.'

'I know,' I said, and told him the problem.

'Why don't you have a Scotch?'

'I don't drink,' I said.

But he bought me a Scotch and all the tension drained out of me.

Now I have a couple each night before bed, but that's all. I still haven't got the taste for it. I still sip a soft drink at meals when others are giving the wine and brandy a seeing-to. Nine years ago I bought a bottle of champagne. It's still in the 'fridge. . . .

Five

During the tough years when money was tight, a number of front-of-house managers would try to fiddle. The worst were the managers of the independent theatres. They got up to all manner of tricks. If the artist was on a percentage of the box office return, there were managers who would play the numbers racket.

In theory, there should have been no problem. One of Johnny Foster's jobs was to collect the returns. Written on the envelope was the amount and the number of people in the theatre, split into circle, gallery and stalls. But my father had a nose for fiddlers. He could smell them. One day at a theatre in Londonderry he looked at the envelope and shook his head.

'Johnny,' he said, 'tonight, I want you to count the audience.'

So he did; it wasn't a long job. 'Seventy in the stalls,' he said. 'Forty in the circle, twenty or thirty in the gallery.' Business wasn't all that good but it was certainly better than it appeared on the returns. The count didn't tally.

The next morning, my father and I went to the manager's office to ask what was going on. We were on fifty per cent of the take. Maybe there were a lot of free listings—tradesmen who got in free for displaying bills in their windows.

We climbed the stairs to his office and saw him through the half-moon window on the stairs that overlooked his office. He had a kettle in his hand and was steaming the Customs and Excise stamps off the tickets so he could use them on the tickets for the next performance. (In those days Customs took a tax on each ticket. The tax was abolished in the 1950s, and I was one of the committee that met with Herbert Morrison to have theatres exempted. VAT has now taken its place.)

'Hullo,' said my father.

The manager dropped the kettle. We had him. Not only was he fiddling us, he was fiddling the Customs as well. From then on, the returns were legitimate.

But there were other ways that managers would screw performers out of their percentages. The manager of a certain theatre in Dudley was particularly sharp. In his theatre, as in some others, the customers bought metal discs instead of tickets, then climbed the stairs and handed them to the usher. There was a brass rail running down the stairs and once the usher had enough discs, he would take the knob off the rail and slide them, unobtrusively, down to the foyer where they would be re-sold. The returns, of course, wouldn't tally with the numbers in the house and so the performer lost out on his money.

Some, however, were on the side of the performer, like the manager of the Tivoli, New Brighton. We played there one winter to rows of empty seats. On the Wednesday night the manager found my father and me in the bar. He looked glum, as if he had just lost a shilling and found a tanner.

'Business isn't very good, is it?' he said, stating the obvious. 'Will you lose money this week?'

We nodded.

'How would you like a guarantee then?'

We looked at him. We were half way through the week. How could he give us a guarantee?

'How much do you get guaranteed?' he asked.

'A hundred-and-twenty quid, sometimes a hundred-and-thirty,' said my father.

'Right,' he said. 'Tell you what I'll do. You give me a tenner and I'll give you a back-dated contract with a guarantee.'

So my father back-handed him and we got our guarantee, which meant that we were all right but the theatre owner was losing out.

At the end of the week my father phoned Wallis Parnell. Val Parnell's brother Wallis ran revues and was following us into the theatre.

'Hey Wallis, are you on a percentage or a guarantee?'

'A percentage,' said Wallis.

'Well don't come unless you get a guarantee.'

'Okay,' said Wallis.

In that sort of way, we all tried to keep ourselves, and our friends, ahead of the game, but occasionally something happened that was totally unexpected ... like broken knicker elastic!

Each Saturday night when the money came in, my mother put it down the leg of her bloomers for safety, but when we were playing the Palace Theatre, Carlisle, the elastic must have snapped. She and my father were taking the curtain call. She bowed and the money fell onto the stage. Quick as a flash, a hand appeared from beneath the curtain and snatched it up. We never found out who pinched the loot!

It was often touch and go, during the Depression, whether we could make ends meet. We played Jarrow when there wasn't a pub or a shop open in the town. The manager of the theatre was giving us a one hundred and twenty pound guarantee and selling two tickets for the price of one. I think we played to thirty pounds that week. Dad couldn't find it in his heart to take the one hundred and twenty pounds, and told the manager to give him just enough to pay the performers— about eighty pounds. The owner was keeping the theatre open because he felt the people were depressed enough with no work, no money and very little to eat.

But when things got bad, there was always Henry Vale to provide comic relief. Henry could be trouble. Sober, he was Mister Nice Guy but drunk he became truculent and could often be downright dangerous. Every so often he would get into an argument with my father and set off along the road clutching his cabin trunk and his homburg. We would run after him and plead with him to come back, grabbing him, standing by the roadside waving our arms. But it was hopeless. Once he had made up his mind, he was off. We would watch him march away into the distance and wonder where he was going. At first we thought he was going back to his wife Eunice Mann, a leading lady in musical comedies, but I don't think he went near her. After a month of so, we would get a postcard from a Salvation Army hostel asking us for his train fare. He would duly turn up at the theatre wearing a morning suit and sandshoes, his homburg on his head and his cabin trunk under his arm. No-one ever knew what he had been up to. We were too polite—or scared—to ask.

He was a tough character. He came with us once to the town hall, Halifax, to entertain at a charity ball. We were playing the Palace and the manager, Wally Stevenson, asked us to perform a cabaret. Wally, a great friend of my father, had a tin stomach. He'd had all his guts taken out and a plate inserted. His party trick was to knock on his belly and make a clunking sound. We were driven from the theatre to the town hall in three official Daimlers. It was mid-winter and freezing.

Once the cabaret was over, Henry, Billy Riley and I made for the women and Henry went on the whisky, which was unusual for him. Normally he drank only beer. He was the sort of man who would be trying to impress someone and he'd be spilling beer down his coat. You couldn't take him anywhere. About two in the morning, the old man told me to find Henry. He was in the Mayor's parlour toasting a woman of about sixty with neat gin: telling her that she was the most beautiful woman he had ever seen. She was blinking at him, one breast hanging out of her evening gown. I pulled him away and got him back to the digs where he went straight to bed in his tailcoat.

I climbed in next to him, went to sleep and woke up at dawn. No Henry. The light was on in the bathroom. I looked in and saw him sound asleep in the bath which was filled to the brim with cold water. He was still fully dressed and his face and hands were blue.

I thought he was dead. I got my father and we heaved him out, stripped him, rubbed him with towels and put him to bed with a hot water bottle on his belly. An hour later he woke up smiling with no recollection of the night before; and no hangover. The man was indestructible.

I particularly recall one night we were getting out of Scunthorpe in about four feet of snow. I was tense. We had played at about thirty quid all week and I was worried about my father, who was due to go to hospital for stomach tests. I was in no mood for Henry. I went down to the station and I was loading the stuff onto the truck when Henry turned up with the second load. He was wearing a cap he had bought in Canada with ear flaps which tied under his chin. His great broken beak was read with cold. He had his laundry under one arm, two bottles of beer under the other and he was in an ill temper.

First, he dropped his laundry between the truck and the platform and had to crawl among the axle grease to find it. Next, he put his beer in a railway carriage on the opposite track and, as he was loading, the train set off and took his beer to Crewe or somewhere. By then he was furious and he began to have a go at my father, saying that the old man was a miser for not hiring a bigger truck.

'I'm fed up with it,' he yelled.

I was inside the mouth of the truck, taking a piece of furniture to bits with a hammer.

'Fed up!' he yelled again and started playing hell with me.

'Henry,' I said. 'I guarantee that if you don't bloody shut up, I'll have you with this hammer.'

I'd no intention of hitting him but he came at me with a right hander, I turned the hammer flat on and clouted him on his cap.

Down he went, out cold. I loaded him onto the cart and took him back to the digs where he woke up in the middle of the night and felt the bump on his head.

'Oh,' he said. 'What happened?'

I told him he fell and he went to sleep quite content. I offered up a silent prayer of thanks for his lack of memory.

His other problem was that he always got involved with the wrong women. He and Billy Riley and I were at a dance hall in Carlisle once, when Henry made straight for the best-looking girl in the place. She turned out to belong to the local gang boss and before we knew where we were we had been bustled out by the biggest and ugliest bunch of thugs in the city. There we were again, back to back, the three of us against half of Carlisle and we must have done reasonably well because for the rest of the week we needed police protection.

That was Henry. He nearly blew away once. We were loading up one night at Burnley and he was drunk again—

always drunk on a Saturday night—on top of a lorry struggling with a ground row—a piece of scenery made of wood and canvas, about six feet by ten. The wind got up and took him off and he flew about twelve feet into the air, like a kite. We thought we'd got rid of him but the wind dropped and down he came onto the platform, quite unhurt. It would appear that there's a God up there somewhere who keeps his eye on the drunks.

Six

When 'Pop Inn' finished, my father was asked by the impresario Tom Arnold to go to South Africa. At first he didn't want to go. The family was his main concern; he hated the idea of breaking us up and it took all Tom Arnold's powers of persuasion to get him to sign. He had only ever been as far as France. The money was good, though, and he made sure that we were looked after by opening a bank account of fifty pounds—a lot of money in those days—for us to draw on if we got in trouble.

I remember when they left. He had been playing the Balham Hippodrome and we waved them off on the boat-train from Waterloo. As the train pulled away, Mona and I felt a bit lost. The family had never been split before. Even when we were playing different theatres, we were always within hitting distance of each other. With my father gone, I was forced to fend for myself.

A woman booker called Mrs Marsden had seen my work with my father and booked me at the Scala picture house, Oxford Road, Manchester, and at another cinema in Preston—three nights at each, at five pounds for each set of performances.

There were two films and I did my act in the intervals—ciné-variety, they called it. I was the only act on the bill, under my own name—Jimmy Jewel. I had worked out an act, starting with a song, 'Annabelle Lee', accompanied on a tinny piano, followed by four or five minutes of gags, then my Jack Buchanan song and dance act; I wound it up with my

Chevalier impression. In addition, I'd pinched a song called: 'Pit Pat, Listen to the Rain' from an American act called Chiltern and Thomas.

I looked out of my window pane
As I looked, it began to rain.
The raindrops as they fell upon the ground
Made this funny pitter-patter sound.
Pit Pat, Pit Pat, Pit Pat....

In between the pits and pats, I did a routine with my feet. That was my act. I opened at the Scala in the summer of 1931, in between Gold Diggers of Broadway, the Pathé news and cartoons. I was nervous but I got a good reception. The audiences for cine-variety were good because they were quite pleased to see a live act in between all that celluloid. It was a break for them, a bonus. I did my songs and my gags—a good opportunity to 'try it out on the dog'—to see how it would go down, in other words. I wasn't too hot on the gags. I'm not a good gag man; never have been. But if things weren't going my way, I could always get myself out of trouble with my Chevalier impression. I did a very good Chevalier. I looked like him and I'd seen him so often that I could almost double for him. Even in Glasgow they loved Chevalier. So much so that, at the Green's Playhouse, they rushed the stage.

I began to pick up spots here and there. I played the South London Palace and doubled at Collin's, Islington, getting four pounds-ten at the Palace and a fiver at Collin's; I played the Hippodrome, Salford—all sorts of places; and I stayed in some awful digs, cold water rooms with outside lavatories; fifteen bob a week and crumpet thrown in—which meant the landlady.

If it wasn't the landlady, then by rights it should have been nobody, because the women who ran the digs didn't approve of their guests bringing girls home. My Uncle Fred had the answer to this restriction. When he invited a girl back, he carried her upstairs, piggy-back, so that the landlady heard only one pair of feet going up the stairs. One night the landlady came out of her room as Uncle Fred was at the top of the stairs. He hid the girl, came down, gave the landlady a quick seeing-to (which is what she was after) and then went back to the girl.

Doing my single act, I worked some of the small places—the No. 3 theatres. The feller who ran the show—usually the comic—paid the acts on a Saturday night. The further down the bill you were, the less you got. Nowadays there are subsistence payments and food allowances but then there was just the wage—a fiver if you were lucky. If the money was bad I would have to 'scarper the let', which meant leaving five bob on the dresser and climbing out of the window with the suitcase in the early hours, like some character in a seaside postcard; I'd spend the rest of the night on the station platform with just enough for the ticket to the next town, ready to go through the whole process again. When I was lucky, I would be allowed to sleep at the theatre, in one of the dressing rooms, to save money on digs; each morning I'd go down to the public baths to wash.

If ever there was a spur to succeed it was the sight of those who were on the way down. Some of the managers were unscrupulous with acts they didn't like. They would put them on before the overture to play to an empty house; they would bill them with the prices, right at the foot of the bill; anything to make the acts break their contracts and walk out. If they were sacked, they had to be paid. If they walked out and broke their contracts, they got nothing.

One way to make a few bob was to put on your own show.

While I was working at the Hippodrome, Eastbourne, a midget called Willie Lancett and I decided to give it a go. Another act, Stoll and Steward, came with us. I brought in Mona and Uncle Fred Marsh. We employed a juggling act and some girl dancers.

We called up some agents and booked a few weeks and I got some of the old man's sets out of the stores. We rehearsed the show at Salford, then opened at the Theatre Royal, Castleford. The show was called 'We're All in it and It's up to our Necks'. After three or four weeks we realised that it wasn't a goer. We finished at the Park Theatre, Bath.

On the Friday night, two men came backstage. They found me in the wings and nodded towards the stage where Uncle Fred was doing a comic act, playing a soldier in the trenches.

'Fred Marsh?' One of them said.

'That's right.'

'We're detectives. He's to appear at Brixton magistrates on Monday.'

'What for?'

'Maintenance.'

Uncle Fred had left my Aunt Queenie and was living with a lovely lady called Nancy. She was wonderful for him and to him.

'You can't take him away,' I said. 'We've got another night to do.'

They were very good about it and we came to an arrangement with them. They took Uncle Fred down to the Bath jail that night and Mona's husband and I went with them. We took fish and chips and sat up half the night with him and the coppers playing cards. The next day they let him out to do the show. The two detectives watched him and took him away again when the curtain came down. On the Sunday I travelled to London with him. He spent the night in Brixton and appeared in court on the Monday. I rustled up the fine for him and got him out. But that was the end of our co-operative show.

Like any young man on his own for the first time, I was learning the peculiar ways of the world. I was playing the Empire, Gateshead, with George Formby as top of the bill. During the show I overheard the agent, who was presenting the bill, ask the stage manager which was the best hotel.

'There aren't any,' said the stage manager. 'You have to go into Newcastle.'

I had digs, a twenty-five-bob combined *chat* up the road. I said he could stay with me if he wanted, so we came back, had a plate of beans in front of the fire and went to bed. About three in the morning he started playing around with me.

'What're you doing?' I was almost completely ignorant about homosexuals in those days.

'Well I was with so-and-so last week at Cardiff and I had it off with him,' he said.

'Well, you're not bloody well having it off with me.' I threw him out into the street. I'd have thumped him if he hadn't gone. I had no tolerance then, none at all, and it's enough to say I never worked for *him* again.

I also learned that there were plenty of sharks around. I had been booked, on one occasion, into a London cinema by an agent called Harry Leet—a fat, greasy man who always wore a felt hat. On the Saturday night I went to his office to collect my wage. He had taken his ten per cent off my four pounds, which was fair enough, but then he said: 'Aren't you going to give me something?'

'What do you mean, give you something?'

'Well, I booked you in here. You've been seen by all the agents. I'm worth more than eight bob to you.'

'What do you want then?'

'A quid.'

I looked at him. 'Do you expect me to work for three pound a week?'

He nodded.

'I'll give you a bloody right-hander,' I said.

I never worked for *him* again either.

Travelling round the country I occasionally bumped into Ben. The family rift which had taken place after that daft quarrel in Doncaster had lasted for more than six years. It was finally healed by an accident to Mona's daughter, Betty. She had fallen from a swing and when she was being treated, she was found to have a tubercular spine. The two families met at her bedside and were reconciled.

I was glad to see Ben after that. He hadn't changed. He was still the cheerful extrovert, going round picking up spots as a blackfaced singer, doing 'Old Man River', 'Walking My Baby Back Home', 'River Stay Away From My Door'. Whenever we met, we swapped stories and occasionally we toyed with the idea of doubling up, just to see how it would work, but it was no more than a vague idea at that time.

One week, while my parents were in South Africa, we found ourselves staying in the same digs in Brixton. We were both looking for work as single acts and we went to the Express Dairy in Charing Cross Road, which was a meeting place for theatricals. An illusionist called Hue Fo Young (his real name was Charlie Pickles) started talking to us. He was trying to get a show together to play a one-night stand at Welwyn Garden City. Could we do a couple of single acts and a double?

'How much?'

'Fifty bob.'

'Each?'

'Don't be silly.'

We took it; but we played straight with him, and told him that we had never worked together before. It didn't seem to worry him. As he drove us to the theatre we worked out a routine, knocked up a few gags. We didn't set the town alight but we didn't get the bird either. On the way back we ran into thick fog. Ben and I had to walk in front of the car all the way from Welwyn to London, some thiry-odd miles. We got to Piccadilly at two in the morning, blew the money on steak and chips at a Lyon's Corner House and walked all the way back to the digs. And that was the end of Jewel and Warriss for two years.

When my parents returned from South Africa, I went back to working with them, preparing and putting on my father's third and final review, called 'Ways of the World'. It ran only six months. Times were too hard. There simply was not enough money to support a full revue with a company of eighteen or twenty people.

It was a dreadful disappointment to have to take the show off—and a bad thing for the performers, naturally. On the Friday night at the Tivoli, New Brighton, an operatic tenor called Norman Woods began to grumble. He was sitting in his dressing room, a big man, heavy and powerful, and madder than a bull.

'The start of the summer season,' he said. 'The worst time in the business. Nobody can get work at the start of the summer season. It's a great time for your father to take off the show.'

I tried to reason with him, placate him.

'We're losing money, Norman,' I said.

He looked at me and without more ado, belted me in the eye. My father heard the noise, burst in and broke up the fight but by the time the scrap was over, I had two black eyes to take with me to Blackpool where I was booked, with my single act, at the Central Pier. The rest of the company looked at me a bit warily as I arrived for rehearsal.

At the end of the season, I was sitting in one of the dressing rooms with a Scots tenor called Donald Reid. He was one of your wild Scotsmen; liked a drink now and then, to say the least. We had been talking about an American dance act in the show, Gold and Ray, and we started talking about dancing.

Donald couldn't dance but he could argue about it. He reckoned that it was possible to do five taps on the wing—tapping your foot five times as you lifted off. I knew better. Henry Vale, after all, had spent months teaching me.

'It can't be done,' I said.

'Course it can,' said Donald.

I showed him, doing a buck and wing.

'It's impossible,' I said. 'Physically impossible to do five taps.'

The next thing I knew, *he'd* belted me in the eye!

The following day I went back home. I hadn't seen my father for sixteen weeks.

'Haven't you got rid of those black eyes yet?' he asked.

I couldn't bring myself to tell him that it was *another* bloody tenor that had clobbered me!

After 'Ways of the World', my father went into semi-retirement. He took over a pub called the Nottingham Castle in Denton, near Manchester, and did occasional spots with his sketches in revues and pantomime. Meanwhile I polished up my own single act. I was ambitious and single-minded. There were plenty of girls around but I had no intention of getting married. I was too intent on my career. I was going to be a big musical comedy entertainer, suave and smooth. That was the plan, at any rate. As it happened, things turned out very differently.

Part Two

Seven

The double act of Jewel and Warriss, which had got off to a false start at Welwyn Garden City, was resurrected by a freak coincidence. In May 1934 I was working the South London Palace and Collin's, Islington, and staying in digs at Russell Square. My father rang and asked me if I was free in two weeks' time. He had been asked to work for a week at the Palace Theatre, Newcastle, and he wanted me to feed him. It was a Fred Clayton and Frank Pope bill. They ran the National Vaudeville Agency and were well-known for offering a six-quid guarantee and small percentage; you got the six quid but you never saw a percentage. I looked at my date book and discovered that I was booked on the same bill that week. I picked up my parents at Denton and drove to Newcastle. We arrived at the theatre and looked at the bill. The coincidence had deepened still further, for there was Ben's name on the bill. We'd all been booked together, but individually, and to cap it all we had been given the same digs.

At band call, on the Monday morning, the manager told us he was in trouble. A Jewish double act called Murray and Cohen had failed to turn up. He needed a substitute to do two spots. Ben and I looked at each other and made a grab for him. Not only would we earn a few more quid, we would also have chance to try out on the dog something we had often talked about doing. We were young and enthusiastic and game for anything. By rights we should never have attempted it but we had the impetuosity of the young. We knocked up an act in the dressing room, pinching every gag we could think of. Right there and then it was obvious that I would be the comic and Ben would be the feed. We never discussed it; it just felt natural. I had done jokes in my act whereas Ben had been the straight singer; and I had a high-pitched funny voice.

We worked out a dance routine to 'Bye Bye Blues', timed ourselves, and found that we had enough for a ten minute act. We went on second spot that night. There had been no time to put us on the bill and there is no record of that first performance. We just appeared, raw and ragged, with our fingers crossed, going into that standard double-act routine.

Ben came on, immaculate in his suit.

'Ladies and gentlemen, I would like to recite "The Wreck of the Hesperus".'

I came on doing a funny run across the stage. 'Isn't it a lovely day to be caught in the rain?' I sang, then disappeared into the wings.

Ben looked into the wings, then back at the audience.

'Ladies and gentlemen, "The Wreck of the Hesperus".'

On I came again, with a funny run.

'Just a minute,' said Ben. 'What do you think you are doing. Can't you see I'm trying to impress the audience?'

I looked at him. 'Have you seen a fella here with a small bowler hat, tail suit and black shoes?'

'No.'

'Blimey. I'm lost again.'

Off.

'Ladies and gentlemen. . . .'

Back again.

'Fifty thousand people at a football match and the pigeon has to fly over me.'

Off . . . back again.

'It's a good job.'

'What's a good job?' Ben is irritable by now. He can't get going with hs recitation.

'It's a good job cows don't fly.'

Off again. . . .

We messed up the odd gag but we felt good together. There seemed to be a certain magic in the combination. The routine may seem dated now but in those days it was standard practice. The impresarios and the audiences expected the straight man to come on and sing or recite something, then get interrupted by the comic; it was part of the music hall tradition. Ben would walk on and I followed him. It took us three years to work out a routine where we actually walked on stage together.

Later in Australia, an impresario called Garnet Carrol looked at our photo and said that the straight man looked like the comic and the comic looked like the the straight man. He had a point; Ben with his big ears and me with my gloomy face, but it worked the other way round.

After the first house, the manager came to see us. He was delighted. Could we do the act for the week and save him getting in another double? *Could* we? We leaped at the chance. We were ready to go. We thought we were off on a new career but we hadn't counted on my luck.

On the Wednesday afternoon we arranged with another act, Charles Dudley and his Midgets, to go to Gateshead and see a film. Charlie, who was six-feet-ten, led his midgets to one car and I ran across the road to my Riley and was flattened by an Austin. I can see it now, the bloody great beak of a stork emblem on the bonnet coming at me. I must have tried to leap over it because the beak went through my leg.

That night, with my leg stitched up, I hobbled onto the stage and did my single act with the aid of a stick. Ben took over from me and fed my father but we were forced to abandon the double act. I should have known. It was the curse of the little red devil again.

At the end of the week we made a decision to team up once we had done our respective summer seasons. I was booked for Llandudno and Ben for Herne Bay. When the season was over we would get together. We shook hands on it. Ben went to Herne Bay and I hobbled off, on my stick, to the Pier Pavilion, Llandudno.

I had done the previous summer season for the person I called the Guv'nor, a nice man called Hugh Stanhope. I was not only the junior lead, but I fed the comic, Fred Gwyn, and also choreographed the dancing girls.

When I told the Guv'nor that I was going to double up with Ben, he played hell with me. He said I had a future on my own. I was on fifteen pounds a week with him, he said, which was good money. Maybe if I went with Ben, I would be back to the cold-water digs and 'scarpering' again.

My father didn't like the idea either. He thought I should stay solo, but for once, I decided not to take his advice.

Ben and I thought that doubling up could be a short cut to the Palladium. All the double acts seemed to be doing well. The Crazy Gang was made up of double acts. There was Connor and Drake, Low and Webster, Murray and Mooney and many others. And so we went to see a revue producer called John D. Roberton. He put on good revues and we had worked for him before. He offered us fourteen pounds between us to do a show called 'Revels of '34', which was to open at the Palace Theatre, Walthamstow, that autumn.

Ben turned up for rehearsals with a girl called Grace whom he had met in Herne Bay. Her parents owned a dancing school and I thought she was okay but maybe a bit toffee-nosed.

'Meet Mrs Warriss,' he said.

He'd got married! I congratulated him hurriedly and we got down to work.

We developed an act, pinching two of my father's sketches—the 'Tripe Supper' sketch with which I had got my first laugh when I was fifteen, and the 'Beefeater' sketch. In 'Tripe Supper', I played my father's part and Ben fed me. In the other, I played the Beefeater and Ben was the little boy who asked me stupid questions.

The first half of the show was variety. Ben did his black-faced singing act and I did my stand-up spot and my Chevalier impression. The second half was a potted revue. This was where Jewel and Warriss came on.

'Ladies and gentlemen. I would like to recite "The Wreck of the Hesperus".'

There we were, billed down among the prices: Jewel and Warriss. There was no question of being Warriss and Jewel. That idea never came up. Somehow it didn't have the right ring.

'Revels' ran through until the panto season. We both worked for Roberton. I did the Syndicate Tour as Buttons in

'Cinderella', Ben played Man Friday in 'Robinson Crusoe'; then we went back to 'Revels of '35'.

We worked along with some good acts, some that were not so good, and some that were downright odd, like Karina, who did an act with a crocodile. It waddled onto the stage and she hypnotised it, stared straight into its little eyes then made it do tricks. The fact was that the beast was spell-bound by a lime light, positioned so that it shone in the croc's eyes. It stared at the light and didn't move. This was okay until one night at the Pavilion, Liverpool, when the lime boy took the light off the crocodile while Karina was working with another animal. It woke up, shook its head and went walkabout. It lumbered into the orchestra pit and I've never seen musicians, before or since, move as fast. The croc cleared the pit in seconds and most of them wound up playing from the front row of the stalls; Karina didn't panic. She leapt after it, grabbed it by the tail and dragged it back onto the stage. Rumour had it that the creature had no teeth anyway.

Then there were the invert teddy bears. Like the invert chimp that attacked my father, they called them the cuddly teddy bears but they were man-eaters, bought cheap because they'd eaten someone. They were unpredictable. They were given stone bottles of milk and honey to drink while they were doing their act, but when they got irritated they would heave the bottles at the trainer.

We made plenty of mistakes but I hope we learned from them. In Dublin, on our first night, I walked on stage in my Beefeater costume. It had a gold crown on the front, the British crown.

'I'm one of the lads that guard the Tower of London,' I sang. 'I guard it night and day to keep the dogs at bay.'

Splat! An orange came out of the audience and hit me.

'Well get back there and guard it,' a voice said. 'We don't want your bloody crowns here.'

Instead of the routine lasting ten minutes, we were off in three. We should have known better.

We also discovered ways of saving money. When 'Revels' came off in April, we had no work and so I phoned the booker for the Synciate Tour, a woman called Florence Leddington who booked us in at Walthamstow for eight pounds a week between us. I had to compere the show and do my single act. Ben did his black-face act and we did two double acts. There were only three other acts on the bill; Marie Kendall who made famous the song 'Just Like The Ivy', her son Terry who did an act with his wife and sister, and a couple of dancers. Ben and I met ourselves coming off stage and going on. All for eight quid between us—except that on this occasion the Friday was Good Friday which we couldn't work, and so she stopped us a pound and all we got was seven.

The next week we were booked into the Argyll Theatre, Birkenhead. We were broke but I knew that on a Sunday it was possible to get 'trip' train tickets for five-bob return, Euston to Liverpool, as against the full fare of twelve shillings single. The snag was that you couldn't take any luggage and we had two enormous cabin trunks, typewriters, radios, golf clubs and suitcases. I said to Ben: 'Here's an idea ...' We were a bit like Butch Cassidy and the Sundance Kid. I would come up with an idea and he would look apprehensive and go along with it.

'Here's an idea ... We buy the trip-tickets, bung the porter five bob to put the baggage in the luggage van and we walk through the barrier with nothing.

As a fail-safe I decided to get off at Crewe, go through the barrier, buy a ticket for Liverpool and get back on the train, so that if there was any query, I'd say I brought on the luggage at Crewe on a normal ticket.

'Okay,' said Ben.

When we reached Liverpool we saw a man in gold braid with two coppers alongside. The guy in the braid was walking up and down the platform with a telegram shouting: 'Jewel and Warriss. Jewel and Warriss.'

The Euston porter had pocketed the dollar then shopped us.

'Jewel and Warriss!' yelled the station master again.

We ignored him and went to the luggage van but he followed us and looked at the labels.

'Are you Jewel and Warriss?'

'Yes,' I said.

'You've travelled on trip-tickets.'

'Oh no,' I said. 'I got on at Crewe.'

'Now lad,' he said, shaking his head. 'They all try that on a Sunday. Come with me.'

They weighed the baggage and charged us thirty-eight bob. Ben glowered at me. We searched our pockets and his wife's handbag. By the time we'd paid up, we had five bob left between the three of us.

'I've an idea,' I said.

'Oh no,' said Ben.

But I went off with my idea to a 'phone box thinking I'd call the old man to wire us a couple of quid to last us through the week.

In those days you had to insert twopence to speak to the operator; once you got through, you'd be told to press button 'B' to retrieve the money. I thumped it, as instructed, and a pile of sixpences and coppers cascaded out. I counted eighteen bob. It was like hitting the jackpot. I didn't have to 'phone the old man. We managed on the eighteen bob until the end of the week when we got paid.

'Revels' ran until the spring and closed at the Theatre Royal, St Helens. Then we were out of work again.

I remembered meeting an agent called Ronnie Blackie when I was doing my single act at the South London Palace— a quiet little man who didn't waste words. In a business with its share of shysters, he had the reputation of being honest.

'I think you have the makings of a good comic,' he had said that night. 'You should forget the Jack Buchanan stuff.' He had turned up again during 'Revels'; and when we were playing Brixton he appeared in the bar.

'Why didn't you come to me?' he asked.

A good question. We decided to try him. I cabled him that we were free and he cabled back immediately with a week of cine-variety: three days at the Canterbury Music Hall, Waterloo, followed by another three at the Blue Hall, Islington. We grabbed it.

The Friday night at Islington was talent spotting night. The management brought in a number of amateurs to mix with the pros, and agents came along to check out the acts. Several of them came backstage after the performance but there was no sign of Blackie.

The next day we went to the Express Dairy in Charing

Cross Road. All the acts went there and swapped gossip. You could find out in a few minutes how everyone else was doing, how well each act had gone down that week, who was getting work, where and when. You also found out which agents or managers were on the hunt for whatever type of act.

That Saturday morning we met Ted Frisby, one half of a black-faced act called Rusty and Shine. Frisby was also a part-time agent and knew everything that was going on. When we came in he winked at us.

'You certainly set the bloody town alight last night,' he said.

'We did?'

'You know that R. G. Blackie's been hunting all over for you, don't you?'

'No.'

'Well, you'd better get to his office straight away.'

So we did an about-turn and went straight there—only a hundred yards away at Cambridge Circus. It was a tatty little office which he shared with the production company of Hope and Palmer. We found him there surrounded by a chaotic mess of papers.

'This,' he said, 'is what I call my W. C. Fields filing system.'

We laughed dutifully and waited for him to continue.

'I hear you did quite well last night.'

Quite well? Everyone else had told us we were bloody marvellous. We discovered later that he had been in the audience, that he had told another agent, Sydney Burns, that he handled us and had made a bet with Burns that we would make the grade before Burns's double act, Syd and Max Harrison (the fathers of the present-day act, Hope and Keen.) Blackie won.

We agreed to let him handle us for six months to see how things went. We shook hands on the deal. Nothing was signed. The relationship was to last for thirty-four years.

An early photograph of Jimmy's mother taken in 1907 when she had just started her career.

Jimmy Jewel's father as the character Simon Shirket in 1914. The costume was copied

Above: The scenery for music hall revues was often extremely elaborate. This set was use before the First World War, for a show in which quick scene changes were needed.
Below: The Jewel family at Morecambe Bay in 1916. Jimmy's father is standing (back ro right) and his mother is seated (middle row, far right). Jimmy is in the front row (far righ

Above: In this scene from the 'Kurios' sketch, Jimmy's father pleads – on bended knee
his mother while Uncle Herbert looks on.
Below: 'Explosions' proved a great success and ran from 1925-7. In the cast were (from r
left) Jimmy, Johnny Foster, Mona, Jack Sheridan, Jack Fentiman, Jimmy's father, Walte
Veedale, Jimmy's mother, Elsie Veedale, Maisie Howard, Audrey Hill, an unknown cha

ny, aged sixteen, with his father

Yours faithfully,
Maurice Marsh

One of Jimmy's most successful early song-and-dance routines was his impersonation of Ja

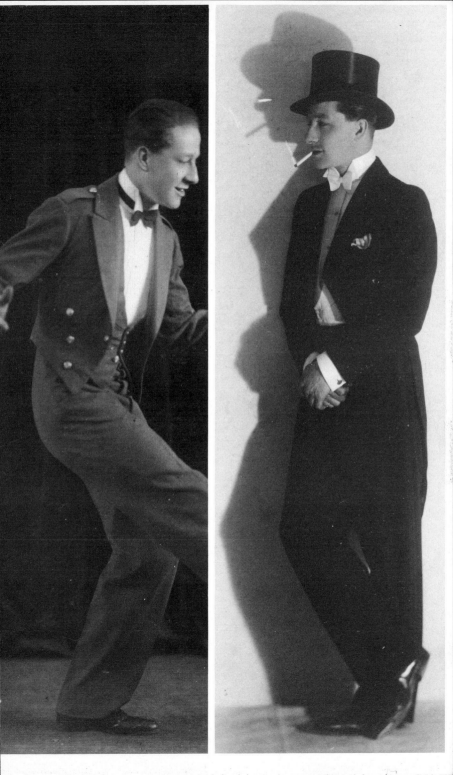

Above: The 'Steeple' sketch was performed at Theldman's Music Theatre; the set was constructed at Salford Stores by Jimmy's father.

Below: In the early 'thirties Jimmy played the Hippodrome Theatre, Norwich with his fa... He is standing on the far right; Henry Vale is standing on the far left; and in the front ro... third from the left, is Johnny sitting next to Mona, with Jimmy's father and mother in the...

Eight

Whenever we had any time out, I tried to get home to see the family. It was no chore, not something I *had* to do, and there was no reluctant sense of duty. I always looked forward to seeing them. I homed in like a pigeon, always glad to be back. I liked Salford. It wasn't the most famous place to live but the people were friendly. We had our local fish and chip shop and the corner grocery shop. It was 'Coronation Street' and I knew all the Annie Walkers, Hilda Ogdens and Elsie Tanners.

Watching 'Coronation Street' today, I can recognise the people I grew up with; one of the reasons for that show's success is that it is so true to life. That was Salford; the world of Lowry and his stick people.

One particular week I was feeling in fine form. We had finished at Hull, and Ben and I had bought a big old Ford for twenty-five pounds. I dropped Ben off at his parents' home in Sheffield and carried on to Salford. I parked the car, bounced into the house and stopped dead in my tracks. My mother and father and Johnny were seated round the fire, all three of them in tears. Even Henry Vale looked glum.

'What's happened?'

'Mona's run off with a guy called Raleano,' said my father.

'Where to?'

'They're playing an if-it show in Biggleswade. The Town Hall.'

My mother butted in. 'He's pawning all her jewellery to get him out of trouble.'

'Right,' I said. 'Let's get down there and sort him out.'

65

Within a couple of minutes I was back in the car. I hadn't even taken off my coat. The old man climbed into the back and Henry sat next to me. It was a silent journey. I felt as if I were driving a hearse. All I could hear was my father sniffing and I stoked up my anger, thinking what I was going to do this Raleano.

We got to Biggleswade late at night and knocked up the night watchman at the Town Hall who gave us Mona's address. It was a room above a shop in the High Street. We got there and roused the landlady. She was a bit disgruntled but she let us in and pointed up the stairs to the door on the right.

As we went up, I turned to my father.

'I'm having no truck with this guy,' I said. 'If he gives me any trouble, I'll give him a right-hander. You get Mona into the car and I'll get the pawn tickets.'

'Right,' said the old man.

We knocked on the door, went straight in and saw them sitting by the fire. Mona seemed surprised to see us, then she smiled, got to her feet and kissed my father.

I ignored her and went straight for the boy-friend.

'Is your name Raleano?'

'Who wants to know?'

'Never mind that. Just get up out of that chair.'

He started to stand up—and never stopped standing up. He was every inch of six-feet-seven. My chin came up to his navel. Nobody had told me that he was a professional strong man. His party trick was carrying pianos on his back, or standing between two cars with a rope in his teeth and stopping them driving off.

'Well then,' I said. 'Let's sit down and talk this over.'

We made the five-hour drive home again, with no Mona and no pawn tickets. Later my father thought about the situation and phoned Raleano.

I was standing beside him, listening.

'Why don't you leave her alone?' he said. 'If she doesn't come back soon, I'll get my son to come and sort you out.'

Who? Me? I thought. No chance; and I hung up for him.

Mona came back when the show finished. As far as I know, nothing much was said. She had gone and then she had come back. The family was complete again.

Times were not good. My father had spent two years working behind the bar of the 'Nottingham Castle', and was becoming depressed. It was hard work with few rewards. The place was a dump and the customers, almost without exception, were bad-mannered bores. It sickened me to see this brilliant man standing behind a counter taking nonsense from these people. It was beneath him and I wasn't having it. One day when he was looking particularly glum, I decided to do something about it.

'You've got to get out of here,' I said.

'I can't,' he said. 'I owe the brewery money.'

'How much?'

'Two-hundred-and-fifty.'

'Forget it,' I said. 'They'll never sue you. It's bad publicity for them.'

Eventually I persuaded him. One night, after closing time I turned up with a hired van and a driver who helped me load his furniture in. I got my father and mother into my little Riley. The old man was grinning when we started off for London.

'What are you laughing at?' I asked.

'I've got my own back on them,' he said. 'I jalloped the beer.'

He'd put Epsom salts or something in the barrels. He grinned all the way to London.

The house in Salford had been let and we shared a flat in Maida Vale. Blackie had booked me and Ben right through that year doing cine-variety. It was hard—five shows a day. We did three shows in one cinema then piled into a coach with the other acts and the orchestra for the next cinema. We all became great card players.

During the Christmas of 1935, Ben and I did pantomine at Cambridge. After that finished we worked in cine-variety at the Trocadero, Elephant and Castle. We did five hour-and-a-half shows between the main film, the shorts and the newsreels, starting at eleven in the morning and going through until eleven at night. For five weeks Ben and I were like moles, seeing daylight only during the journey to the cinema in the morning.

Meanwhile my father was appearing in panto in Manchester for a man called Jack Gillan. My mother had stayed in London and he was living in the house in Salford with Henry Vale. There was no heating in the house and he let himself get run down—he wasn't eating properly either. He got a bad chest cold and had to leave the show after three weeks and come back to London. He was feeling bad and he had this idea that if he rubbed his chest with camphorated oil or sat barefoot in front of a blazing fire till his feet burned, then the cold would disappear.

There he was, sitting toasting his feet and I was rubbing his chest with camphorated oil. I tried to cheer him up by telling him it was possible to light a fart.

He said: 'I don't believe it.'

I said: 'You can.'

He said: 'Well, show me.'

So I did and he laughed and it was the last laugh he ever had.

He went to bed that night and never got up again. The cold turned to septic pneumonia. We called a doctor in but he was involved in a car crash and ended up in hospital himself.

Father was ill for nine days—hallucinating. He became briefly lucid at one stage and said to me: 'Don't let the sharks get at your mother.' He meant the solicitors. Then, in his last conscious moment he said: 'Jim, look after your mother.' Half an hour later he died in my arms. It was 23 January 1936. He was just fifty-five.

I had always felt that he was indestructibe. I could not absorb the fact of his death. I can't remember much about the next few weeks. Until the day he died, I worked with my mother on his sketch, 'Daring Experiment' at the Queen's Theatre, Poplar, doubling in cine-variety at the Trocadero, Elephant and Castle. When he died, my mother went to pieces. I carried on working the Trocadero, followed by the Grange Cinema, Kilburn. I don't remember the audiences or anything about the act. I suppose I was like a boxer getting up from the canvas, carrying on purely by memory and blind instinct. Ben and I were committed to five shows a day but I remember nothing except a numb blackness.

Nor do I know much about the funeral. It has been wiped clean from my memory. Only two flashes of recollection remain. The first is Henry Vale breaking down on the drive back from the cemetery at Willesden Lane, Kilburn.

'Why him? Why the Guv'nor?' he said in tears. 'That's the Guv'nor back there.'

The other memory is of Val Parnell who came back to the flat with his wife Dolly after the funeral. I'll never forget his last words to me.

'You're the man of the house now. Try to be like your old man. He was one of the most respected men in the business. Try to live up to him.'

He also offered me help and advice; there and then I decided I would go to him for advice only on matters that did not concern my career. Val Parnell was a very powerful man and it would have been easy to ask for his help but I wanted Ben and myself to make it on our own. It was important that he came to us when we were ready for the big theatres like the Holborn Empire and the Palladium. This happened, but not for another few years.

Although I didn't register the fact, George V died the same week and the whole country was in mourning. At one point during that nightmare, someone put a cigarette in my mouth. I had never smoked before and I've never stopped since.

I count the years working with my father as the golden years of my life. In the ten years since I had first come on in the pit sketch to deliver a telegram, I learned a lot about the business and also about human nature. I could sing, I could dance, I could play pantomime, do a somersault, hand-springs, flip-flaps, tootle on the sax, feed sketches, do my stand-up routine and impressions. But above all, I was in the privileged position of being son to a man of such good grace. For as long as our little touring company had lasted, we had been our own bosses—or rather worked for a boss we knew and loved and who shared our lives.

The condition of the variety theatre in those days was not all that good and we often played in towns that were all but ruined by the economic climate. But we belonged. We were a family—the family unit of Marshes plus the larger group of those who worked with us and shared the ups and downs.

Each one of us was dependent on the common sense and decency of the Guv'nor.

He was decent and he was caring. Little incidents proved it—like the day he drove from Salford to London to see me. He had been told (wrongly as it turned out) that I had contracted VD. We sat on a bench in Leicester Square and he told me where we were going to go to have the condition cured.

'But I haven't got it,' I said.

He could have 'phoned to find out, but instead he made a round trip of four hundred miles. Yet, a year or so later when he was going to see Val Parnell, I didn't help him. His coat was a bit threadbare and he asked to borrow my new one. I refused. I was going up to the West End to see a girl and I wouldn't let him have it. To this day I regret being so insensitive. It was a small thing but it still haunts me.

One incident summed up his attitude to the rest of us. In 1927–8 he was called to London by Clayton and Waller, the leading theatrical managers of the time and offered a part in a new musical called 'Hit The Deck'. He was to play the comedy lead opposite Ivy Desmond. He had consistently turned down work for anyone unless my mother and sister came along with him. He always insisted on a package deal. This time he asked for a small part for Mona. The management refused and so he turned down them down.

After the interview we all had lunch with him at the pros' meeting place in Leicester Square, a place called Jones Corner House. I was thinking that he had thrown away a golden opportunity. He was still running his revue and wouldn't take it off out of loyalty to the company. I looked up and saw a comic called Syd Howard coming toward us.

'Sit down,' said my father. 'How's business?'

'Bad,' said Syd. 'Worse than bad. Terrible. I think I'm going to have to pack it in and go back to being a house painter.'

Without hesitation my father told him about the part he had just turned down and persuaded Syd to go along to Clayton and Waller. The part had gone to a comic called George Bass but Syd got the role of understudy. When Bass fell ill, Syd took over and became a big West End star.

If, as I think, my father turned down fame and fortune out of loyalty to his family, then such an act was consistent with his nature. In all the time I knew him he never said a harsh word against my mother and she in turn was a great influence on him. They were very much in love. He was one of the very few men I have known in the profession never to have had even a fleeting affair with another woman and he engendered in me a passion for family ties and close bonds. I remember so much about him that was glamorous and exciting but what I remember best was his determination that we should look after one another, no matter what. Towards the end of his life he paid the price.

During the Second World War, the house in Salford was bombed. My mother and my niece Betty were sheltering in the cellar and it took a day to dig them out. When I got there and saw that they were safe, I talked to the surveyor who said that the stores had been hit by the blast and that the building had to come down. For the next three week-ends I drove from Edinburgh where I was working and packed all the scenery into lorries to be taken to London.

On the last Sunday, I stood and watched as a team of men started to pull down the stores. I was heart-broken. The building held so many memories of my father and I could see him standing in front of the paint frame with a huge sheet of canvas in front of him, a paint brush in his hand, unshaven, a cigarette in his mouth, his cap on his head, overalls streaked with paint. I thought of all the hard work he had put in and I cried unashamedly. The stores had been part of him and his life. The scenery made in them had been his creations. Images of him and the things we had said and done flashed through my mind as if I were watching a film, and I thought that when he was born, they broke the mould. There would never be another one like him.

I still miss him terribly. During the war I went with a group of people to see Jimmy Cagney in 'Yankee Doodle Dandy' in the West End. The story is based on the life of George Cohan, the performer and song writer. There is a scene in the film when Cohan's father dies and the family is gathered round the bed.

71

It was so like my father's death that I broke down and had to sit in the men's toilet until the film ended. I've seen the film since on television and it still affects me after all this time.

What makes the pain harder to bear is the knowledge that only three weeks after he died, the sulphur tablets M and B came on to the market—tablets which would have saved his life.

Nine

Soon after my father died, Blackie booked us into a show
called 'Lucky Stars', a big revue produced by a company
called Hope and Palmer. It was an extravaganza. Bessie Love,
the American film star, was brought over to head the bill.
There was Sid Seymour and his band, Jane Eyer and Eddie
Leslie, a dancing act called Anita Charles and Jack. There
were sixteen dancing girls and fourteen lorry-loads of scenery.

And there was Jewel and Warriss, way down the bill in
small type, doing our usual front of cloth gags and dancing
and the 'Beefeater' sketch.

The show opened at the New Cross Empire and played all
the Moss Empires theatres. This was the premier tour and we
felt that at last we were on our way; playing the No. 1 theatres.
We were cocky. We had it made. We were given ten minutes
for our first spot—the gags and dancing—and eight minutes
for the second spot—the 'Beefeater' sketch. If anyone did a
minute over or under, a report was sent by the manager to
head office and the offender would receive a letter of
complaint, asking why the act had been either expanded or
reduced.

We were doing fine until we reached the Glasgow Empire,
graveyard for English comics. We just about got by on our
first spot but they didn't want to know about the 'Beefeater'
sketch. They just stared at us. An eight-minute comedy act
allows about three minutes for laughter. If they don't laugh,
you're in trouble. Instead of doing eight minutes, we were off
in four. The theatre manager was through the pass door like a

tornado. He had been an army officer and he tore into us as if we had deserted under fire.

'Not only have you done under your time,' he roared, 'but in my opinion, you're act isn't worthy of Moss Empires. And I'm putting that in my report.'

Sure enough when we got back to London to play the Finsbury Park Empire, we were summoned to head office in Leicester Square and asked for an explanation.

We saw Cissie Williams, who was Val Parnell's assistant. She had the manager's report in front of her and she tore a strip off us.

'But they didn't laugh,' we said weakly.

'You're paid to make them laugh....'

But I think she realised how tough it was. The Empire was notorious. And she didn't threaten us with the big stick of 'you'll-never-work-for-Moss-Empires-again'. That sentence put the fear of God into any performer because Moss were big and if they didn't want you, then you went down the bills fast.

The Glasgow Empire knocked a bit of the cockiness out of us; we were a bit like the young fighter who thinks he is great, then gets knocked out and realises that perhaps he is not so good as he thought he was. We learned our lesson.

But we still had ideas of our own. When we worked for John Roberton we realised that he was making money by renting out scenery and putting on shows. Why did we need him, we thought? We could do it just as well ourselves. If he can do it, we can do it.

I went to see Alfred Esdail and Charles Clore, who had an office in the Prince of Wales Theatre. I'd known Alfred for years. He had been a friend of my father.

'What do you want?' he enquired.

'You hire out scenery to John Roberton,' I said, 'Ben and I would like to do the same—put on our own shows.'

'And how are you going to pay for it?'

'Out of the returns,' we said happily.

'But we're in business. We need money up front before we hand out scenery.'

'We've got no money,' we said.

'Then get out of my bloody office.'

Yet another lesson; but still we tried. At the Aston

Hippodrome, Birmingham, the cast began going on in each other's acts after the fashion of the Crazy Gang and we more or less turned our act into a Crazy Gang show. There was a comic and face-puller called Alec Pleon, and Al Marshall, an eccentric dancer. We were enjoying ourselves and one night a young dancer suggested we join him and a few others and put on our own show. He said it should be called the New Young Bloods of Variety and should be based on the Crazy Gang formula. We would do it on the 'if-it' and share whatever profits we made. We thought it was a great idea and called up Blackie to see what he thought.

'Forget it,' he said. 'You're getting twenty-five pounds a week. It's a terrible idea. The guy's a lunatic. He doesn't know what he's talking about.'

And so we turned the young dancer down. His name was Bernard Delfont—now, of course, Lord Delfont.

'Lucky Stars' ran for nine months and we played every major theatre in the provinces. I toured my mother with me. She had not got over the death of my father and was hitting the bottle quite hard. She didn't normally drink a lot but a couple of Scotches would make her maudlin and aggressive. I thought that it was better that she came with me rather than stay alone in London. Mona had gone back to Johnny and they were staying in rented rooms. There was no room for my mother there. The Salford house was let to several different families; and so I kept her with me.

She cramped my style a bit with the girls. A lot of them thought I was queer or a mother's boy. There were times when I was just getting going with a bird backstage and my mother would appear, slightly the worse for wear. Instead of taking the girl home, I'd have to take my mother.

Ben and I were earning twenty-five pounds a week between us, less ten per cent commission. A couple of bedrooms and a sitting room in pro digs cost two pounds a week and most landladies would do you all in for two pounds ten shillings a week per person and so we just about made ends meet. I had a little Renault two-seater on HP which cost eight pounds. Petrol was eleven pence ha'penny a gallon, which was cheaper than travelling by train. Occasionally we picked up a Sunday concert to supplement the wage. One Sunday we travelled from Birkenhead to Tynemouth to earn fifty shillings. After paying for travel we came out with a pound profit which meant we could have a game of golf. We didn't complain. There were many who were worse off.

After 'Lucky Stars' we did a summer season at Bridlington for my old Guv'nor, Hugh Stanhope. In between shows we watched a young girl doing impressions in the open air in front of a band. It was hard work for her but it was obvious that she had a lot of talent. Ben and I looked at each other and nodded in agreement. She had the talent to succeed if she got the breaks. We checked her name—Beryl Reid.

In the spring Blackie told us that he had an offer for us to tour Australia. We were to take over from an act called Connor and Drake in a show called 'This Year of Carnival'. We wanted to do it but there were complications. Ben had just set up home with Grace and I was having problems with my mother, who was missing my father more and more. She would abuse me for no reason then go walkabout, just take off and walk the streets and I would have to go out and search for her. I was afraid that if I left her behind she might neglect herself or even commit suicide. There was only one thing for it I would have to take her with me to Australia.

I was pretty depressed. We had managed to cancel most of our dates in order to make the trip, but we were committed to some cinema work.

I was sitting in a café between shows at the Prince of Wales Cinema, Harrow Road, and looking glum. Ben looked at me and asked what I was going to do in the week off.

'Paris,' I said. 'I'm going to Paris for three or four days.'

I don't know what made me say it. I had no intention of going to Paris until I opened my mouth.

'I'm going on the Saturday night boat-train,' I added. I didn't even know if there was such a thing as a Saturday night boat-train.

'If I don't get away from the family,' I said, 'I think I'll go barmy.'

'All right,' said Ben. 'I'll come with you.'

'You can't do that,' I said. 'What about Grace?'

He sat in silence for a minute.

'I'll tell her I'm going to have a few days with my mother and father in Sheffield.'

'You're bloody mad,' I said. 'She'll find out.'

'No she won't. They're not on the 'phone.' Now he was warming to the idea. 'I'll send the old man a couple of letters to post to her from Sheffield. . . .' So that was that. I was committed.

We went down to Victoria and, much to my amazement, there was a Saturday night boat-train. We got on board and we were in Paris on the Sunday morning. It was the first time either of us had been abroad and we wandered around open-mouthed like a couple of hicks. An act from the Prince of Wales, Harrow Road, had given us the name of a hotel and we thought we were in luxury. The room had its own bathroom attached, which was heaven to two fellers who were accustomed to cheap digs and outside lavatories.

We wandered up to Montmartre and stood outside a house with a red light outside. We stood there for a long time trying to pluck up courage to go inside, counting our francs. Finally, we made our entrance. Inside were twelve girls in various stages of undress.

'How much?'

The answer was too much. We were about to leave when the madame called us back.

'Okay then how much can you afford?'

Business must have been bad because we produced a pound each and were led off. We didn't get over the experience for a long time.

Ben and I arrived home on the Monday night and the following week I picked up Ben and Grace from their flat in Bayswater to drive down to Colchester for our next show.

'Did you have a nice time in Paris?' asked Grace.

'Yes, thank you.'

'Was it all it's cracked up to be?' asked Ben.

'Oh yes.'

And I had to go through the whole thing with Ben asking questions all innocent and curious.

I dropped them at their digs and we kept up the pretence all that week. But the following week, when we were playing the Old Hippodrome in Aston, Birmingham, Ben turned up one night with a face like an open grave.

'What's up?'

'Grace has left me,' he said. 'When we got to the digs she asked me point-blank if I had been to Paris with you and I couldn't tell a lie.'

'You're crackers,' I said.'

'Of course, she blames you.'

'Oh that's bloody charming, that is.'

She'd gone back to Sheffield to Ben's parents, so I wrote to Ben's dad asking him to tell her it was nothing to do with me; but I always felt that she felt the whole thing was my fault. It wasn't the first time I got the blame. Or the last.

Ten

In April 1937 we left for Australia on a ship called the *Jervis Bay*—me, my mother, Ben and Grace, together with an act called 'The Two Rogues'. The *Jervis Bay* was an immigrant ship and most of the passengers were on assisted fares at five pounds. Although we were paying the full fare of fifty, there was no discrimination. All the bunks were the same. The ship had originally been built to carry horses and the stalls were converted into cabins. I shared a cabin with one of the Rogues for the six-week trip. At first the food wasn't so bad but by the time we were three weeks out, we were sick of it.

In Valetta the ship was refuelled by coal barges which meant that everyone—and the food—was covered in a fine layer of coal dust. Sheffield seemed a long way off.

We arrived in Melbourne, checked into the Arcade Hotel and went to the Prince's Theatre to look around. The company had decided against the expense of bringing chorus girls from England and was auditioning local girls.

Ben and I watched from the stalls and Ben pointed out a tall red-head.

'How d'you fancy her?' he whispered.

I did. I certainly did. Her name was Belle Bluett, a member of one of the best known show-business familes in Australia. The father, Fred, had been a highly successful comic and Belle's brother Gus, who had recently died, had been the most versatile of the lot. They had a saying in Australia:

'Our bridge, our Bradman, our Bluett, our harbour.'

Anyway, I was keeping my eye on Belle and I heard later

79

that she had taken an interest in me—an interest that waned for a time because she saw me going around with a woman. She asked who it was and was told 'Mrs Jewel', and assumed my mother was my wife.

The cast was made up of George Duncan the principal comic, two American acts—the Blenders, a close harmony act, and the Dawn Sisters—the Damorra Ballet, the Two Rogues and us. We were warned that the Australian public would not tolerate dirty material and that on no account were we to use anything remotely suggestive.

On the first night George found his opening spot wasn't going too well, so he slipped in a dodgy gag.

'There's this old feller of seventy-five married to a girl of eighteen,' said George. 'Nothing happened in the marriage for a long time until one night when she felt old age creeping up on her.'

It wasn't exactly Lenny Bruce material but it was enough for the show to get a bad press. The bad notices—together with an epidemic of infantile paralysis which kept people indoors—meant that our ten-week run folded in three weeks; that screwed up the schedule and so the company sent us to New Zealand.

Meanwhile Belle and I had been going out together. I was becoming very attached to her. It quickly became obvious to both of us that this was more than just a casual affair. The problem was that the Bluetts were the Royal family of show business and I was forever being warned by stage hands not to take liberties with 'our Belle'. They all got the same two-word reply.

I discovered that, like the people at home, the Australians had their own tricks. I found out about the 'water tour', by which the bookers—if they didn't like an act—would send it for three days to Perth, then to New Zealand for another three days, then by boat again to Tasmania—after this routine, most acts would tear up the contract and ask to be sent home. They couldn't do that to us since we numbered over twenty people; but we did get moved around and laid off for long periods.

Ben didn't help matters either. On one occasion he gambled

with our wages in a poker game, and lost.

'It's only money,' he said. Ben was easy-going.

'*Our* money,' I said. But he just grinned and let me do the worrying for both of us. In fact, he let me do the worrying for thirty years.

While we were in Christchurch we received a cable saying that Mona had died of a brain tumour. My mother was inconsolable. She blamed herself for coming on the trip and spent her time fretting about my niece Betty. It was a terrible shock, coming so soon after my father's death, especially as we had no idea that she had been ill. I had gone to see her just before leaving for Australia. She was living in rooms in Manchester with Johnny and working in an awful pub. I couldn't understand why she was working such a place because she was a brilliant comedienne. She'd started to drink seriously at that time.

I had asked her if she was alright, if she and Johnny were happy and she nodded. But I left with a little misgiving. Something was wrong. The tumour must have been growing in her head even then.

We were in Australia and New Zealand for a year. We played golf on the last course in the world in a place called Bluff, where South Pole explorers kept their sled dogs. We drove through parts where there were no trains and we played tin sheds wherever there was an audience; places like Westport, Blenheim, Nelson; and Pickton, which was just a hall with a stage at one end about two feet off the ground. They dug a hole for us in the front of the stage and placed the piano in it, so that the pianist had to sit on the floor with his legs in the hole. There were two rooms at the back of the stage. The girls dressed in one, the men in the other. There were no flys and we couldn't use scenery so we had to make do with drapes.

Then there was Invercargill, a dry town, but even so I'd never seen so many drunks lying in the gutters in my life.

We left New Zealand and went back to Sydney for Christmas and played in $112°$ in a theatre called the Mayfair which had no air conditioning. The stage manager was a man called Lew Shafts, a nasty big bloke, all of fourteen stone. I'd already had a row with him which had resulted in a Kiwi called Kirk Yates, a six-foot-four-inch prop man, throwing Shafts into the orchestra pit.

I suppose it might have been the heat but there was always the chance of tempers getting short. We did a sketch called 'Bare Idea' which was a skit on nudity. I played a butler and wore only underpants and a bow tie. Ben and Dave McMurray, one of the Two Rogues, played burglars in cloth caps and underpants. One evening, Dave forgot his cap, so as he went on, he took a cap off the head of one of the stage hands. When he came off, the stage hands were belligerent and Shafts, in particular, was making a big thing out of it. Ben got wind of the trouble and did a runner, vanished through the front of the house. When Dave and I left through the stage door, there were five of them waiting for us.

Shafts grabbed Dave, who was five foot nothing and said: 'If you ever *** do that on one of my *** stagehands I'll knock your *** head off.' Then he hit him, with an uppercut which lifted him off his feet.

I said: 'Don't do that', and straight away he started on me. I must have been doing all right because the four stage hands joined in and I finished up against the wall with all of them having a go at me.

Just then, the stage door opened and rescue arrived in the shape of Belle who started laying about them with her handbag. As soon as they realised I was Belle's bloke, they backed off. Like I said, the Bluetts were well respected. The the manager arrived and Shafts was made to apologise. I think it was at that point that I realised that Belle was the one for me.

In Melbourne it was becoming obvious that the show was not a huge success. We hadn't had a good press and the management decided to cut its losses. The rest of the acts were paid off with full salary for the six remaining weeks of the contract but we were told that we could play a tour of working men's clubs in Sydney with half our salary being paid by the clubs and the other half by Fuller's Theatres—either that or we could take half salary and go home. Although we knew that the others had been paid in full, we decided to cut our losses, take half the money and go. But first we had to do a week at a place called Bendingo—cine-variety again.

82

Bendingo was a gold mining town about one-hundred-and-fifty miles from Melbourne. They hadn't had rain for two years and it was 120° in the shade. There was no water except for drinking and that was brown when it came out of the taps. On top of that we arrived in the middle of a firemen's convention. They came from all over the state. There must have been five thousand of them. They held torchlight processions till three in the morning and they slept where they fell. We shared a room in a pub with three of them who came in at all hours, drunk out of their minds.

The cinema we played at showed a film with Joe E. Brown called 'Fireman Save My Child'. The firemen would come in and fart at the picture, then when we came on they did the same to us.

We finished there on the Friday and were due to sail for home from Melbourne at noon on Saturday. Belle joined me for the last two days. We asked for an alarm call at six but didn't get it. The taxi driver woke us and we dressed in the cab and just made the Melbourne train. If it wasn't for that taxi driver we might still have been in Bendingo. We reached Melbourne at eleven-thirty, got a cab to the dock and just made the boat. Belle and I had decided to get married and I just had time to kiss her goodbye before the ship sailed. We had agreed that we would marry as soon as I could afford to send for her, though I had no idea when that would be. It was an emotional moment as the ship moved away; I realised how much I would miss her.

The trip home took six weeks. When we docked at Southampton there was a telegram waiting for us from Blackie saying that we were to open that night at the Hippodrome, Aldershot. We got the boat train to Waterloo and my mother broke down completely, thinking about Mona. Ben's parents met us at the station; there were floods of tears and she went away with them. She was going to stay with them until I could get her back to Salford and re-unite her with Betty. As I watched her go, Ben tapped my arm. It was noon. We were due to go on stage at six. We had just enough time to get on a train for Aldershot, then rush to the theatre, give the band parts to the conductor and get ready for the first evening performance.

Eleven

We were back in the old routine of cine-variety again at twenty-five quid a week between us, hoping that the Big Break would come. It didn't. Ted Gollop, a booker for Moss Empires, came to see us and reported back that we were a cross between Murray and Mooney and Dave and Joe O'Gorman, two well-established double acts, and that we were not worth more than twenty-five quid. However, a couple of weeks later Moss Empires asked us to do a cross-talk spot in a show called 'Hollywood, Harlem and Home' at the New Cross Empire. Apparently the Moss Empires people thought that there wasn't enough strong comedy in it. We agreed, although this meant that we had to double at the Granada, Woolwich. We did the afternoon show at Woolwich, dashed the five miles to New Cross, did the first house, dashed back to Woolwich, did two shows, then back again for the second house at New Cross.

After the second house at New Cross, Val Parnell walked into our dressing room. He was the chief booker with Moss Empires at that time.

I was always rather in awe of him. He was my godfather. I first remember meeting him when I was nine. At that time he was a minor booking agent for General Theatres Controlling Ltd, one of the No. 1 tours in the country doing the Hippodromes—Brighton, Birmingham, Southampton, Newcastle, Liverpool, Manchester, Sheffield, Bristol and a few theatres in London. He was a great friend of my father, an immensely big man, over six feet and very handsome with an overwhelming personality and dynamic energy. Even as the years went on, and I began to think of him as a second father, I never lost my initial awe for him.

My father once said to me: 'You have just met a man who will one day either control or own a great chain of theatres.' He was right. Val became managing director of Moss Empires and later managing director of Associated Television.

He was working hard to bring the life back into the theatres. Those that had been in the doldrums were being refurbished, the old pit orchestras augmented by new musicians and the variety formula changed. Instead of the old idea of six or seven acts, Moss Empires introduced quick-fire variety with no act doing more than seven or eight minutes. Val travelled to the continent and twice a year to America to book acts for the London Palladium and a subsequent tour, providing new blood for show business and bringing back the audiences.

He came into our dressing room that day and shook my hand. I hadn't seen him since my father's funeral.

'Where the hell have you been? he asked.

'Australia,' I said.

'Why haven't you been working for us?'

'Because your booker doesn't think we're good enough,' I replied.

He said nothing, just turned on his heel and left. Within a few minutes he had called our agent and asked us to do a spot in the second half of the show. So, now our daily routine looked like this: the afternoon show at Woolwich, first house at New Cross, back to Woolwich for one show, back to New Cross to do the second spot in the first house, back to Woolwich for the last show, then back to New Cross for the second house—a total of five journeys and seven appearances a day. It was worth it, though. Blackie told us that Val Parnell had booked us at the Hippodrome, Wolverhampton, the following week at thirty-five pounds. We were on our way. We'd cracked it at last!

I sent for Belle, somehow rustled up the forty pounds for her fare. She arrived when we were playing Finsbury Park Empire. We talked about getting married, but decided to wait until she had seen a bit of the country and knew that she would be happy here.

85

Meanwhile other people were getting interested in us. Blackie called and said that an American agent called Charles Tucker wanted to see us. Tucker had been a violinist who had married into the Lyons food family, given up his fiddle and had become a big agent. We went to his office, Blackie, Ben and myself.

He was squat and bald, well-dressed and very American— and he didn't waste any time.

'Look Blackie,' he said. 'I want to buy the boys' contract off you. I want to handle them. I'm prepared to give you five thousand pounds.'

We didn't know that amount of money existed; we looked at Blackie with our mouths open. Blackie was in terrible trouble at the time. He had only us and two other acts on his books, the finance company had just repossessed his car because he couldn't keep up the payments and he was behind in the rent on his office. The temptation must have been enormous but he was a very honourable man.

'I don't have a contract with Jimmy and Ben,' he said. 'We have a gentleman's agreement.' But we told Blackie that we wanted to stay with him. We felt that, if the breaks were coming us, then Blackie had been responsible for them and deserved any commision. So we turned Tucker down and wandered into the sunlight wondering what the hell we had done.

The next week I went to Blackie's office and found it bare. He was packing his papers into cases. 'Have you had the bailiffs in?' I asked.

He shook his head. 'They must want you pretty badly,' he said, and explained that he had done a deal which would involve him working for Tucker as general manager and splitting the commission on his acts. That was Tucker's way of doing things. Because Blackie wouldn't sell us, and because we wouldn't leave him, he bought a package deal. It was a move that proved very fruitful for all of us.

Soon we made our first appearance in the West End, at the Holborn Empire with Max Miller topping the bill, followed by a show for Tucker called 'Tops Every Thing' with Leslie Hutchinson, the Maurice Colleano Family, Max Wall, an American girl trumpeter called Olive White and sixteen girl dancers. The show opened at the Hippodrome, Birmingham then went on tour.

One day during the tour, Tucker told us that George Black had come back from America with material he had bought from Abbot and Costello. We met Black and he said that he would sell us the routine which was called 'The Hole in the Wall' or the 'Mustard routine'. The price was two-hundred-and-fifty pounds and the deal was that our salary would be raised by twenty-five pounds a week and the money transferred to Black until the two-fifty was paid off. He told us to go and learn the material which we would use in a show called 'Black and Blue' at the London Hippodrome. We were to use the sketch in three weeks' time at the Empire, Leeds for two shows only, to break it in and Black would be sent a report by the theatre manager on the audience reaction to it.

We read it and it was marvellous. We broke it in on New Year's Eve 1938 at the Empire. Max Wall, who was also to appear in 'Black and Blue', stood at the back of the running tabs with the script to prompt us in case we forgot the lines but we had it word perfect and it got one belly laugh after another; yet there were no gags in the routine. It was dialogue, like a play, and the timing had to be perfect.

Ben started it off by saying: 'Isn't this a beautiful theatre?'
I said: 'Yes.'
'That's a lovely wall over there,' he said.
'Yes. Smashing wall.'
'Suppose you go over there and bore a hole in the wall.'
'Alright. I'll go and bore a hole in the wall.'
'Why should you go over there and bore a hole in the wall?'
'I'm not boring a hole in the wall. You said: "Suppose you go over there and bore a hole in the wall." I don't want to bore any holes in the wall at all. If I want to get out, there are doors I can get out of.'
'Alright. Forget the hole in the wall. Suppose you were at a football match. Who's playing?'
'I don't know who's playing?'
'What are you doing in the ground then ...? Alright, forget it. What's the first thing you do when you get there?'
'Buy a ham sandwich without mustard.'
'Oh. Mustard and ham go together.'

'Well, let them go together. I don't want to stop any romance.'

'Because you don't like mustard, we should close all the mustard factories and put all those people out of work ...?'

And so it went on. Bent logic. He twisted everything I said.

'Suppose you're on a bridge?' he said. 'And you jump off.'

I said: 'I'm not jumping off any bridge.'

'Well, what are you doing on the bridge?'

'I'm not on the bridge.'

'What were you doing in the football ground?'

'I don't know. You got me in there now you can get me out again.'

... and I got more exasperated.

The audience loved it. Instead of running for eight minutes as George Black had said, it ran for fourteen.

He got the report and told us to do it again at the Palace Theatre, Hammersmith on the Friday night and said that he would be in the audience. Friday is a bad night for the theatres. People don't go. When he came to see us, it was a particularly poor audience. There were six people and a pigeon out front and the material died on us. We heard nothing from him but we had the consolation of knowing that we were to use the sketch when we opened in Brighton with 'Black and Blue'.

Meanwhile we were still performing in 'Tops Everything'. One night Max Wall was held up by fog and missed the first house and the manager asked us to do an extra routine. We suggested that we do the 'Hole in the Wall'.

'You can't do that,' he said.

'It's only for one show,' we argued. 'Black and Blue' opens here in a couple of weeks and we'll be doing it then; but in the meantime one show can't make any difference.'

'That's not the point,' he said. 'Vic Oliver and Enid Lowe are going to do it.'

We were stunned. Not only had the material been taken from us, but we were no longer booked in the show. George Black never had any intention of giving us the material. All we were doing was acting as guinea pigs, testing it out for Vic Oliver. On top of which we had left our date book open, so we were out of work.

It would be an understatement to say that we were disillusioned with Moss Empires; and it took us a long time to get over it.

Meanwhile, at the end of the 'Tops Everything' tour, Max Wall decided to get married. Belle and I had been sharing digs with him and he was becoming a big star. I have always considered Max a genius; he could do everything. But he was always in trouble with women.

He had decided, finally that he would marry a girl called Marion Pola but Max's mother, Stella, whom he thought the world of, was against it. She called me and asked me to come to her house in Staines. Max was due to pick up his possessions, she told me, and would I look in and persuade him not to get married?

'He's at least thirty years old,' I said. 'I can't do that ...' But I agreed to go and see them. When I got there, Stella was in bed, surrounded by Pekinese dogs. Her new husband, a guitarist called Bill Tringham, was sitting in the lounge.

Belle and I were talking to Stella when we heard a commotion. Max had arrived and there was a fight going on between him and Bill. I ran in and got between them but just as they both sat down, Stella arrived in her nightdress and began to whack Max. Even as we got him out of the house with his suitcases she followed, throwing stones from the rockery at us. Finally she went back in and I followed her to say good bye. She was sitting on the bed, cross-legged. She looked straight at me, pointed her finger and said in a dramatic voice.

'You traitor! You Leopold!'

Leopold? She was thinking of Leopold of the Belgians who had recently capitulated to the Germans.

I scarpered fast and never saw her again.

For the summer season of '39 we were booked into the Regal Theatre, Southend. We rehearsed constantly because we were changing programmes twice a week. At that time we finished our act with a song and dance; Ben sang 'Goodnight Sweetheart' and I clowned around, eating a banana and rolling up his trousers. But we felt that we needed something new as a finale, something a little different.

There was a song going round called 'Timber':
Timber, timber,
Can't you hear us a-calling for timber.
Swing your axe you lumberjacks
Timber's got to come down the river today...

That was the opening lyric. I thought there must be something we could do with it. One Saturday I went out and bought what seemed like a hundredweight of firewood and on the Sunday, Henry Vale helped me to make a couple of boxes. They were three feet by two and hinged at the bottom. When a pin was removed the bottoms of the boxes swung open. We filled them with the firewood, tied them to a batten and pulled them up over the stage. I had a tin helmet which was going to be used in the act. I put it on, stood under the boxes and told Henry to pull the rope that would release one of the pins.

My God! I didn't know what the hell had happened. There was a clap of thunder as the firewood fell. I staggered round the stage and the manager, who was the only other person in the theatre literally fell off his seat, he was laughing so much. After I'd recovered, I realised that we couldn't do the gag in tin helmets so I got a felt hat, stuffed a towel in it, and went back to stand under the second box.

Timber, timber...
Timber's got to come down the river today.
Crash!

For a second I thought I'd been poleaxed, but the effect soon wore off and I realised we'd got a great finish to the act. All I had to do now was convince Ben.

When I told him at Monday's rehearsal he looked at me as if I were mad, so I showed him the trick and forced myself to smile, pretending that it didn't hurt. He fell about laughing and wanted to try it but I didn't let him. If Ben were to feel the wood crashing down on his skull, he would have backed out straight away. But I thought that, if I could get it to work in front of an audience, the the sound of laughter would make up for any discomfort.

That night as usual I was sick with worry, wondering if it was a good idea—panic-stricken in case it didn't work for some reason. Ben and I had rehearsed the song and we were both standing under the box on our chalk marks. I could see

Henry Vale holding the rope and grinning at me.

Timber, timber...

Timber's got to come down the river today.

The firewood came down and it got the biggest laugh I'd heard for a long time. Ben just stood there for a moment stunned, then he turned to me.

'You bastard,' he whispered.

But the laughter was so sustained that he had time to add: 'They must all be sadists. Listen to them.' And the curtain came down.

The timber gag had been a success and got us back with Moss Empires. Three weeks later Val Parnell saw us at the Gaumont, Holloway and gave us a tour on the strength of the 'Timber' routine alone.

Twelve

It was beginning to look as though war was inevitable and it was time for Belle and me to make a decision. She had been in England for a year and the question was whether she should go back to Australia until it was all over. She decided that she wouldn't go back. The war could go on for years, she said. And on 31 August 1939 we were married at Southend Registry Office. Henry Vale was my best man and Fred Gratton, who was also in the current show, was one of the witnesses. Neither Ben nor my mother was there. They thought we were already married. It seemed easier that way. Belle and I had been living together with my mother and it had been diplomatic to pretend to be man and wife. My mother was dead against the marriage. Somehow in her mind, it meant the break-up of the family. I never told her about the real date of the marriage; I told Ben later but my mother never knew.

Henry Vale turned up in a pullover, old grey flannels and plimsolls. Our wedding breakfast was a cup of coffee and a bun at Lyons, then back to the theatre to do the first show. It was hardly the sort of thing romantic young girls dream of; nor was the honeymoon, come to that. It was delayed for a year until we had a week out. I hired a caravan and a car and drove down to Salcombe in Devon. Henry came along too. I don't know why. He was always around. He'd always been with us, so he came along. I don't think Belle liked the idea very much. Henry wanted to sleep in the caravan but Belle wouldn't let him. She said his feet smelled too bad, and much to his disgust he was forced to sleep in the car. He couldn't understand it. I think he was quite upset.

The very day that war broke out, Belle and I were on our way north. We thought that London was going to get bombed and that the north would be safer. We took a train from Southend to Euston and were caught in the first air raid alert of the war. The sirens went and we scampered down into the Tube Station for ten minutes. It was a false alarm; and in any case it didn't worry me as half as much as the news that the theatres were closing down because of the war. I was beginning to think I would never work again.

My mother had started taking in lodgers—mostly dockers who were a rough bunch but, on the whole, kind and generous. I was broke. My worldly savings—thirty pounds—were in a building society but, again as a result of the war, there was a moratorium on withdrawing the money. I went for a job as a lorry driver but never got started. Then a wire arrived: from Ben saying that the theatres had re-opened and that we were booked into the Palace Theatre, Plymouth on the following Monday.

The problem was how to get there. My mother helped out with the fares but we still did not have enough and eventually one of the lodgers made up the difference. But for him, Jewel and Warriss might have ended their careers there and then.

The journey took fourteen hours. The train was blacked out; there was no heating and nothing to eat; and finally we arrived in Plymouth at midnight with nowhere to sleep. I remembered having stayed in a digs there with my father when I was about fourteen but all I recalled was that the house was opposite the theatre. Miraculously, we found it. A frail old lady answered the door. I asked her if she had any rooms and she looked at me closely.

'I know you,' she said. Your father was Jimmy Jewel and you stayed with me when you were a boy. You set fire to my curtains.'

But she let us in. The only trouble was that she was deaf and if we ordered bacon and eggs for supper, we'd find a plate of beans and chips. We tried leaving notes for her but that didn't work either. She couldn't read.

It was a difficult start to the war years but, as it turned out, these hard times were to be the beginning of a success story for

us. Plymouth was followed by the Gaumont Cinema, Holly-
way where Val Parnell saw us again, liked the 'Timber' gag
and booked us.

We played the East End during the Blitz and for over a
month we barely slept and hardly ever had a bath. The sirens
would go when we were in the theatre and we simply carried
on the act till four or five in the morning, dredging up all the
old material and improvising; anything to keep the audiences'
minds away from the bombing. Once the all-clear sounded,
we would get back to our digs in Chelsea—a terrible place.
We slept at daybreak and kept the curtains closed. The one
time we opened them, we were treated to the sight of bugs
running up and down the walls.

Eventually the managers of that theatre had enough and
decided to close down. We were quite relieved. We'd heard
that the Hippodrome, Aston was open and first got a booking
there, followed by one in Bristol.

Meanwhile Alfred Esdail who ran the Prince of Wales
theatre and had taken a keen interest in our career offered a
long-term contract going up to two hundred pounds a week if
we left Tucker and Blackie and worked under his management.

We told Blackie about it and eventually, after much
negotiation we decided to stay with them if Tucker could get
the 'Hole in the Wall' material for us. He wrote a letter to this
effect and we later used the material, in pantomime in
Edinburgh thinking that the letter cleared us. It was during
our Edinburgh performance that the BBC decided to record
part of the act. At that time, the whole of the Moss Empires'
staff had scarpered out of London away from the bombing to
Great Missenden and radio was their only entertainment. Of
course they heard us doing the routine and next day George
Black sent us a cable saying he was suing us, the BBC and
Howard and Wyndham. Eventually the whole thing was
settled and we sent George Black a cheque for fifty pounds
which brought us the 'Hole in the Wall'.

Then we headed north to Glasgow to play panto at the
Theatre Royal for Stewart Cruickshank, the managing direc-
tor of Howard and Wyndham. We had mixed feelings about
Glasgow. I remembered playing the Green's Playhouse, doing

my Chevalier impression. They loved it and rushed the stage, but Ben and I had died at the Empire and we were never quite sure what would happen. Glasgow could be very dodgy. I remember playing the Metropole in one of my father's shows, when I did a song and dance act dressed as an American sailor.

I sang the first verse of 'I'm going back to Emmezaz, Emmezaz the pub next door.' When I got to the dance chorus, the trumpeter stood up to play his solo. He was well into it when the bell of his trumpet was hit by a penny thrown from the Circle. Without hesitating, he put down the trumpet, climbed out of the pit and vanished up the aisle. I carried on warbling until I heard a commotion in the Circle—and there was the trumpeter grappling with the penny-thrower. He picked the feller up, heaved him over the parapet into the stalls, came back, picked up his trumpet and carried on where he left off.

That was typical Glasgow. Not for nothing was the Empire known as the graveyard of English comics. They might go for Chevalier but English comedy could go down like a lead balloon.

They loved the American acts and the Scottish comics but they didn't laugh at us. We were on the bill with Max Wall at the Glasgow Empire in 'Tops Everything' in 1940. Max went on and somebody blew a raspberry. Max moved forward and put his foot on the footlights.

'Louder,' he said.

Brrrp!

'Louder!'

Brrrp!!

'You're no good,' said Max. 'I've had it from bloody experts.'

And still they didn't laugh. There was no way you could win them over. Ted Ray said they couldn't clap because of the steel filings in their hands. It was rumoured that they ate their young . . . and Des O'Connor was once dying so badly that he threw a faint—pretended to collapse on stage just to get off.

But in panto at the Theatre Royal that year, we did well. Top of the bill was Dave Willis and the press review was: 'The two Sassenachs, Jewel and Warriss fight a far from losing battle with Dave Willis for top comedy honours.' Which, from the Scots, was praise indeed.

Stewart Cruickshank, the manager of Howard and Wyndham's theatres, was so pleased that he signed us for three pantomime seasons at rising salaries of eighty, ninety and a hundred pounds a week. He also offered us work in his 'Half Past Eight' summer show, which was an honour because previously he had used only Scots comics.

It was these long-term contracts which enabled us to get deferment from the services, provided we did ENSA tours.

I was pleased. I didn't want to go into the Army. I wouldn't have been too good at taking orders. If someone had told me to get a haircut, I'd have probaby thrown a right hander. Anyway, Ben and I felt that entertaining the troops was as important as being in the Army. We were a couple of morale-boosters.

When we came back I tried to locate Henry Vale. Ever since the Australian trip I had been finding work for him, either as a stage manager or as a feed for us. He had been working as stage manager for Alfred Esdail in 'Gaities de Montmartre' but when the show finished its tour, Henry vanished for the last time. There were no postcards from Salvation Army hostels. He never again turned up with his homburg and his cabin trunk. He simply vanished off the face of the earth. Even now I think of him and wonder what became of the man.

Everyone, of course, has his war story. Mine is playing an ENSA show at Chatham. We were appearing at an Ack-ack site by the dockside when the bombers arrived to attack the warships. We were in a Nissen hut, the men dressing in the sergeants' mess, the women in the next room. At the first explosion I called out to Belle to take cover, grabbed my fox terrier Max (named after Max Wall) and dived under the billiard table. When the all-clear sounded, Belle stormed in and had a go at me for being more concerned about the dog than her. There was little protection in the woman's room and Belle had spent the raid under a card table.

We were beginning to come good by now with a full date book and a contract for six weeks in Cruikshank's 'Half Past Eight' show at the King's Theatre. We stayed, in fact for twenty-seven weeks.

Blackie kept calling and asking when we were coming back to civilisation. Finally he booked us back with Moss Empires at the Hippodrome, Wolverhampton. He wanted to know how much money to ask. We thought about it for a while. Our top money with Moss had been thirty-five pounds a week. Ben looked at me and shrugged. 'To hell with it,' he said. 'We're coming back to Glasgow panto. Why don't we ask for a hundred a week.'

So we wired Blackie, expecting to get a rude reply. Instead he wired back that we'd got the hundred. It was something of a milestone and we permitted ourselves a small celebration. Tommy Trinder was top of the bill and we did two spots. I think we made it hard for Tommy because we did really well. We had developed a piece of material where I kept saying to Ben:

'Carry on 'Arry Boy.'

Why I called him Harry I don't know. It wasn't funny in itself but it became a slogan. Tommy stole it and later we almost came to blows over it.

After Wolverhampton we went back to the Lyceum, Edinburgh for Stewart Cruickshank in 'Half Past Eight', but the show was not so successful as Glasgow had been. The Edinburgh audiences wanted their own Scots comics. After twelve weeks, Cruickshank came to us and said: 'It's no good. We're taking the show off.'

We were depressed about it because it was the first time we had been taken off. We phoned Blackie from the North British Hotel and told him the bad news.

'I'm glad,' he said.

'Eh?'

'Val Parnell wants to put you in 'Gangway' at the Palladium. What's more, Tommy Trinder is going to make a film and he wants you in with Ted Ray.'

We were ecstatic. The Palladium was everyone's ambition. From being fed up one minute we were now raring to go. We finished at Edinburgh on the Saturday, caught the train to London and immediately started rehearsals.

We thought we would need a new set of clothes for the Palladium so we went to a tailor called Cyril Castle who made us two dinner jackets for twenty pounds and two lounge suits for fifteen each. We looked immaculate but Ted Ray looked a bit tatty. He never spent money on clothes. I looked at him as we were waiting to go on.

'Where did you get your suit Ted?'

'Hawes and Curtis.'

'Thanks for the warning.'

He didn't speak to us for two months after that.

The show opened on August Bank Holiday 1942 with a matinée. Val Parnell and a director called Robert Nesbitt were out front.

Before the show started Ben and Ted and I stood at the side of the stage waiting to make our entrance. We were all nervous; I had been almost sick with the tension. As we stood there, Val Parnell came through the pass doors and put his arms around us.

'Good luck,' he said. 'There's no-one worrying but you.'

It was exactly the right thing to say—it calmed us down.

After the show Val and Robert Nesbitt came back-stage to congratulate us. It was the first time we had met Nesbitt. He looked at us and said:

'Just one thing. Don't wear white socks with dinner jackets.'

That night we heard George Black was in the Royal Box. He was the biggest impresario in the business but we weren't sure whether he thought we had any potential. George Black was the typical cigar-smoking impresario, a man with a great knowledge of what the public wanted.

After the show, we were sitting in the dressing room when we heard feet on the stairs, then George Black came in, puffing, out of breath and full of praise. He said the 'Timber' routine was marvellous. He apologised for the confusion caused by the 'Hole in the Wall' material.

Ben and I grinned at each other. Not only had we made the Palladium, but we had made a success of the Palladium. Now came the hard bit. We had reached the peak. All we had to do was stay there.

Thirteen

Stealing or 'knocking-off' material was common practice in show business. There is no copyright on routines. I believe you can put your own material in a registered letter and send it to yourself and have some security in law, but I don't know anyone who has done that. And although Ben and I did our share to get started (it was the only way to get on for an unknown, to knock off gags) we soon stopped once we had enough material of our own and it used to make me mad when it was done to us; not by up-and-coming youngsters but by the established acts.

When Tommy Trinder knocked off our 'Arry Boy stuff, I was angry. I arranged to meet him at the Variety Artists' Federation offices to discuss it.

'You can't claim it,' he said.

'Yes I can,' I said, 'because you worked on the bill at the Hippodrome, Wolverhampton. You watched us do it and then you did it at the Palladium.'

He got a bit aggressive with me and if I hadn't been stopped, I think I would have thumped him. He subsequently cut it out of his act but we couldn't do it at the Palladium and I was very upset. We're the best of pals now of course. It's all water under the bridge, but at the time, my right fist was cocked for action.

We also had the timber gag knocked off—by an English comic who used it in Australia. He was a Lew Grade client. I phoned Lew and complained but he said I was being petty. The fact was that if ever we went out there again, we wouldn't be able to use the routine ourselves.

There wasn't much you could do about that sort of poaching. Towards the end of our career we were working Pontin's Camp at Morecambe. The manager there, a young ambitious bloke, saw our wedding routine and sold it later to an act called Lester and Sharp. We found out about it when we were all on the same bill. We were closing the show and I went out front to watch the first half and there they were doing our routine, the material that we were supposed to be going to follow them with! I had to rush back to Ben and tell him that we'd have to change to another routine. I collared them about it but they said they had bought it from the manager at Pontin's; they seemed to think there was nothing we could do about it.

Some people weren't as tolerant as we were though. There was a double act called Nervo and Knox who did a slow-motion boxing or wrestling act and another duo knocked it off. One week when they weren't working, Nervo and Knox went and watched them, then waited for them outside the stage door. They said, 'You've knocked off our act.' The other two started to argue, so without more ado, Nervo and Knox gave them a belting—which was no more than they deserved.

It happened all the time. There was an English comic called Al Burnette who went to America, watched Milton Berle, came back and did all his gags in the night clubs. He looked a bit like Berle. Both had big, hooked noses. I was in New York when they met at a Lambs Club function. By this time Berle had had a nose job done. They were introduced. Berle looked at him and said: 'I know you. You're the guy who works all my old material. And what do you know—you've got my old nose.'

If you weren't being sabotaged from inside the business, there were those outside who could clobber your act. Watch Committees are local councillors, often women, who used to scrutinise each act for any blue material or innuendo. We didn't use anything blue: we didn't believe in it; but some of those women took censorship to a ridiculous length.

Birmingham was notorious. You almost couldn't say *boo*! Glasgow wasn't too bad, but then you didn't get any laughs in Glasgow so it didn't matter much what you said. In Glasgow the fire-prevention people were even worse than the Watch Committees. Although we fire-proofed all our clothes and pieces of scenery, they would still come round with blow torches and try to set the bloody things alight.

We had a sketch in which a load of hay fell down on us; four big bales of hay; and for Glasgow we took the bales, found baths in No. 1 and 2 dressing rooms, stuck the hay in the baths and let it soak all day.

The fire-prevention officers came in an hour before the show. The hay was soaking wet but they wouldn't pass it.

'What can I do?' I said. 'The sketch depends on the hay.'

'Vegetables,' said the fireman. 'Drop vegetables.'

So, out I went in a car and bought up half the vegetables in Glasgow—cabbages, cauliflowers, leeks, the lot. And there we stood in the middle of the Empire with tons of assorted veg dropping on us.

In all fairness, I ought to say that most of them were polite enough; but one fireman in Glasgow went too far. I was standing in the wings smoking (smoking was part of the sketch). He came past and slapped the cigarette out of my mouth. I levelled one at him and, in return, knocked his false teeth out. It caused one hell of a row. The stage manager told me that if I didn't apologise and buy him a new set, the curtain wouldn't go up for the second performance. So I said 'Sorry' and promised to pay for his teeth.

The fire people were also very careful with one of our props, a Model T Ford which stopped and started on its own. It worked on a time switch powered by a windscreen wiper motor with six pedals to control the various effects.

We would fire a revolver at it and that would seem to get it started. We took off the steering wheel and it still went round the stage on its own. At the end of the act, when the driver finally got in, the back would fall off. It was some car, but like any other it needed petrol. The fire-prevention people allowed us only enough petrol for the four minutes of the act—which meant we couldn't afford too many laughs unless the act ran over time. If that happened, we had to push the car off stage at once.

One night at Bristol I stopped the car in the middle of the

stage and we got out and did our usual dialogue about the car running out of petrol. But as he was climbing out of the car Ben accidentally stood on one of the pedals. After thirty seconds the car started up; but instead of remaining stationary, it took off across the stage knocking down the scenery together with a few people in the wings. Fortunately no one was hurt. Someone dropped the curtain and the scenery was hastily rebuilt. But it occurred to me that if the car had been pointing the other way it would have run into the orchestra pit and might well have wiped out half the band!

Looking back, it seems there were so many things to overcome. If your material wasn't pinched and you got past the Watch Committees and the fire-prevention people, there were still other hazards.

Many of the managers were little more than glorified office boys. They were treated as little gods by their staffs but in turn they were terrified of their own bosses. If they heard that one of the hierarchy was coming in, it was as if the Gestapo were on the way. They would fuss around telling us to make sure that we didn't run over our time.

'V.P.'s in Front,' they would say. Or 'G.B. or Cissie Williams.'

If the show ran just a minute more than it should have, they were through the pass door like tornados telling you off.

If fussy mangers, firemen, and thieving comics weren't enough to put up with, there were also spies; not the wartime Mata Hari version, just little men and women whose job it was to keep a sly eye on the performers. Ben missed a Monday rehearsal once at the Hippodrome, Brighton and I had to cover for him. I said he had a cold. Three weeks later we were discussing a sketch with Bob Nesbitt—we were not sure whether it was okay to mention the black market in the dialogue.

In the middle of the discussions Val Parnell walked in.

'Do you think it's dangerous for Jimmy and Ben to talk about the black market Val?' said Bob.

'No,' said Val. 'But will Ben be there to take part?'

'What d'you mean?' said Ben.

'You didn't turn up for rehearsal at Brighton,' said Val.

'I was poorly,' said Ben.

'You weren't bloody poorly,' said Val. 'You were up in Glasgow with the girl you're going to marry.'

They had spies everywhere.

Fourteen

The Palladium show 'Gangway' was followed by a twelve-week ENSA tour followed by 'The Big Show' for George Black in Blackpool which took us through the summer of '43.

Our career was going along well. It was a bit like those scenes in old musicals when a train roars along the tracks and the names of the towns are superimposed to show constant upward progress.

Blackpool was followed by a tour with 'Black Vanities'—a big show and the first time anything like it had been tried. We played three weeks in each town and the last week was invariably the best, thanks to word-of-mouth enthusiasm.

We were on two hundred pounds a week with 'Black Vanities' but we were later scheduled to play in pantomime for Stewart Cruickshank at half that salary. Our eight-week run at the Theatre Royal, Newcastle broke all records and at the end of it Cruicky came down from Edinburgh and asked us to do another three years for him.

We met him for lunch at the Royal Station Hotel and told him that we would love to work for him but that we had other commitments.

'How much were you getting with 'Black Vanities',' he asked.

We told him.

'So you must have lost a lot of money coming out of the show.'

'That's right,' I said. 'But a contract is a contract. And anyway it was because of you and the success of 'Half Past

Eight' in Glasgow that we managed to increase our fee with Moss Empires.'

He looked at us and nodded. 'Who's the girl in the "Push Off" sketch,' he asked.

'My wife Belle,' I said.

'Who pays her?'

'We do.'

He didn't say anything, but the following week we received a letter from him thanking us for the wonderful business that we had done in Newcastle. Enclosed was a cheque for Ben and me for seven-hundred-and-fifty pounds and another for Belle for twenty-five pounds.

Cruicky was unique. One of the first gentlemen of the business, and often complimentary about our act. There were others, though, who would bring us down to earth. We had a week spare when we were working for Cruicky and we were booked into the Theatre Royal, Barnsley. We were full top of the bill and getting one-hundred-and-fifty pounds; bottom was Billy Scott Coomber with his Singing Scholars. One of the Scholars was a lad of ten.

This ten-year-old murdered the audience. They loved him. We went on and died on our feet. We did the 'Timber' routine and no-one laughed.

At the end of the week, the manager, a man called Mitchell whom I had known since I was a child, came in to our dressing room to pay. He began thumbing out the fivers onto the table:

'Five, ten, fifteen, twenty, twenty-five....' He paused. 'Tha'll never be as funny as tha father,' he said. 'Thirty, thirty-five, forty...'

At this time, Ben had married a beautiful soubrette called Meggie Easton and almost immediately we were off on another ENSA tour, to the north of Scotland.

We were in a digs called Erchlas Castle. From the outside, it was a fairy-tale place, all turrets and cornices, like something out of Disneyland. Inside, behind the great stone walls, it was freezing.

When the ENSA people took over a place, they installed their own staff and instead of landladies, we had ENSA 'matrons'. Some of them were quite military and were very conscious of regulations. One weekend Ben and I had been given a couple of fillet steaks by a butcher but the Matron would not cook them for us. It was official bean pie or nothing and so we had to sit in front of the fire with a pair of forks trying to grill the bloody things like toast.

The Matron at Erchlas Castle was a nice woman but she knew the rules like the rest of them. Ben and I had bought a couple of spaniels and the Matron took one look at them and shook her head.

'No dogs in the castle,' she said.

'But they're in the show,' Ben said quickly. 'They do jokes.'

'All right then,' she said reluctantly.

All was well until the day she announced that she and her husband were coming to see the show. Again we had to be fast on our feet. We slipped a song into the act called 'Trees', just for that one night.

I think that I shall never see
A poem lovely as a tree.

The stage hands, as rehearsed, threw the dogs on and they wandered around the stage looking lost. But the Matron was satisfied.

And so war continued; variety and pantomime punctuated with ENSA tours. We did the 'Big Show' at Blackpool, and headlined with Tessie O'Shea. It was a big success, marred only by the death that summer of George Black. His sons took over the production and Val Parnell was made managing director of Moss Empires.

We got on well with Tessie. We did a sketch called 'Anglo-American Relations' in which Ben and I played Tommies. I was the gormless one again and Ben had to tell me how to get going with the girls. Tessie played the girl I was chatting up. At the end of the sketch Ben carried his girl offstage and I was meant to carry Tessie. But at rehearsal I couldn't lift her. She was about fifteen stones. I tried the fireman's lift but couldn't get my arms round her. Joan Davis, the dance director, suggested the obvious thing. It got a big laugh, Ben carrying Zena Dell off and Tessie carrying me . . .

I remember the day the war with Japan ended. A group of

us were eating in a Greek restaurant in Blackpool when the news came through. Everyone went crazy. I thought it would be a good idea to get Ben in on the festivities, so I drove to his digs and tooted the horn. He opened the door and bawled me out for making a noise and didn't wait to be told that the country was finally at peace. He just slammed the door.

The war was over, but the shows had to go on—and so did the search for new material. George Dorman, who did a footballing act on unicycles with his brother Jack, told me about a sketch he had seen in America where a pianist played the Anvil Chorus and stagehands threw horseshoes at him.

'Do you mind if I use it?' I asked.

'Go ahead,' said George. 'It's not my idea.'

'What happens after they throw the horseshoes?' I asked.

'Nothing,' he said. 'That's the finish.'

I thought it could use some additions, so I worked on the idea as a burlesque of Rawitz and Landaur who were very big at the time.

I had two prop pianos made and we expanded on the idea. After the stagehands had thrown the real horseshoes at us, we threw others made of felt into the audience. After the second verse, someone threw a horse's harness at the piano and broke its legs. A cock crowed through the mike, then a hen walked on. We put the hen in the piano. Then came another verse; the cock crowed again and an egg fell out from under me. Finally a carthorse came on. The only problem here was that when it saw the lights and heard the orchestra, the horse always got stage fright—and the result of that was invariably embarrassing.

On the last night of the show at Blackpool a friend handed Ben and me two golf balls a-piece over the footlights. It might seem an odd thing for him to have done but golf balls were like gold dust at the time. You couldn't get them for love or money. After the show George Dorman turned up in my dressing room, rather drunk. I thanked him again for giving us the idea for the routine and handed over the golf balls as a token of my appreciation.

He thanked me and stumbled off to Ben's room. I wondered why he was going to see Ben, because they weren't the best of friends.

107

George knocked on the door and went in.

'Look what your partner has given me in exchange for the "Anvil Chorus",' he said.

'Very good,' said Ben. 'And here's two more to go with

Ben handed him his golf balls. George took them and then, without any warning, whacked Ben on the chin. God knows why. Down he went. I heard the thump, rushed in with another member of the cast and dragged George away.

Once we'd got him outside, we talked to him and calmed him down.

'Okay, sorry,' he said. 'I'll go back and apologise.'

'You're not going to start another fight?'

'No.'

He turned, went back to Ben's room and immediately whacked him again, so I ran in, belted George and pulled him back into the passage.

A week later a meeting of the Water Rats was called to sort out the incident. Both Ben and George were Water Rats. I wasn't a member but they asked me along as a witness. I turned up at the meeting and found that the blame had been placed firmly on my shoulders.

That seemed to be my role: always taking the blame while trying to sort things out. Once we were up in Leeds, with Ben Lyon, and decided to play some golf. Ben picked us up because he was never short of petrol. He worked a lot for the American forces and had plenty of coupons. On our way to the links, a Bentley cut up Ben on a roundabout. Now, Ben had a short temper. He chased the Bentley, caught it at the next roundabout and pulled over to block it. We got out, the two Bens and I, and from the Bentley appeared four fellers— all very big men. So the two Bens backed out and got back in the car and I was left there in the middle like a fool. I had to talk my way out of it—do a lot of apologising.

Once more records were broken when we appeared at the Empire, Sheffield. Later we worked with Val Parnell on plans for his first Palladium production after George Black's death. The show was called 'High Time'. Ben and I, Tessie and Nat K. Jackley were the headliners. We did the Rawitz and Landaur sketch, the Anglo American sketch, and a double talk routine that ended with 'My Blue Heaven'.

It was a spectacular show. It opened with a scene where the chorus girls dressed in all colours of the rainbow. Ben and I wore rainbow coloured dinner jackets with straw hats and sang 'Pennies from Heaven' while a collection of huge silver pennies was dropped on us. The first half ended with the 'Timber' routine incorporated into a saloon scene in which Tessie played the hostess and we threw dollar bills into the audience with her face on one side and our faces and Nat Jackley's on the other.

The show got rave reviews. We had been together for twelve years and we could now consider ourselves at the top of our profession. We were earning two-hundred-and-fifty pounds a week.

One night a little man called George Inns knocked on our door at the Palladium. He was a radio producer. Would we like to do a radio series, he asked.

We had done the odd broadcast but we didn't know much about radio. We had never worked with other people around a microphone but we were well aware of the power of the radio set. It had made national names of Arthur Askey in 'Band Wagon' and Tommy Handley in 'ITMA'.

The BBC gave us an existing show to work on called 'Navy Mixture' with Charmaine Innes, Benny Lee, Paddy Marks (Alfred Marks's wife) and a singing group called the Key-notes. We did thirteen shows, either recording on the Friday afternoon at the Paris Cinema, Lower Regent Street, or at different venues on a Sunday afternoon. The Friday shows were more of a problem because it was difficult to get a studio audience at noon on a Friday. One day, when the time came to record, we had only ten people out front and so George Inns and I went out to grab an audience. We saw a group of people walking down Regent Street and went up to the leader.

'How would you like to see a radio show being produced?'

'Very much. Thank you.'

They all trooped in and watched the show in silence. The place was like a monastery; I was reminded irresistibly of the Glasgow Empire. When it was all over I approached the man who had led them in. 'Didn't you like the show?' I asked.

'Oh yes,' he said.

'So why did no one laugh?'

'Laugh?' he said. 'They didn't understand a word. They're all Polish tourists: I'm just taking them on a tour of London.'

Just after 'High Time' opened, Belle went home to see her mother. I felt terrible seeing her off at Euston on the train to Liverpool. I didn't know how long she would be gone. The boat took seven weeks to get to Perth and I couldn't get in touch with her during that time. I received one letter from Durban saying that she had been sick during most of the voyage, then a cable from Perth. The ship's doctor had discovered that she was pregnant. I cabled her to leave the ship at Perth and fly on to Sydney, which she did.

I was delighted. We had not long before moved into our flat—the first home we could really call our own and I was excited about the prospect of having children. On the other hand, I didn't want her to be away for too long. I got in touch with the airline and found out that she couldn't travel back after she'd become more than four months pregnant. She had intended to stay for six months, but in fact she returned after six weeks. Some friends went down to Poole Harbour to meet her from a Sunderland flying boat and brought her straight to the Palladium. It was a highly emotional reunion.

'High Time' ran until the end of February 1947 and just before it closed, our son Kerry was born. I stayed at the nursing home in Bentinck Street until the birth and I couldn't wait to phone Ben and then get to the theatre to let everyone know. After the show I took all the cast to Olivelli's, an Italian restaurant in Store Street, and we drank toasts to the baby.

So 1946 had been a wonderful year for us. We had been a big success in 'High Time'. We had broken into radio and now I had a son to follow me in the business just as I had followed my father.

After 'High Time' finished, we did an American show for Emile Littler called 'The Red Mill', which had originally been produced in 1904 and had recently been seen on Broadway. It was the story of a double act which had somehow become involved with the aristocracy. We read the script and liked it. There were some great songs in it, but we thought that the location should be changed from New York to London: that the show should be anglicised. Emile Littler agreed and brought in script writers and musicians to make the adaptations.

We opened at the Opera House, Blackpool and played for two weeks to capacity business then moved to the Lyceum, Sheffield with the same success. When the show moved to London, though, the reviews were a lot less than friendly.

We opened at the Palace Theatre, Cambridge Circus at the same time as 'Oklahoma' which got smash reviews. By comparison ours were mild. The critics said that 'Red Mill' was rather dated. Another thing that went against us was Emile Littler's decision to invite the Press into the office at the interval and feed them booze. Instead of a fifteen-minute break, the interval lasted half an hour and by the time the second half opened, the audience and the Press had lost interest. The notice to close went up at the end of the first week and we ran for only two.

But if that was a mistake, we soon came across an idea which added another dimension to our act. It was the work of little George Inns again. He came to see us with a radio series called 'Up The Pole'.

Hindsight can be a distorting mirror but it is nonetheless tempting to look back on 'Navy Mixtures' as an excellent training ground for 'Up The Pole'. 'Navy Mixtures' was no great success but it gave Ben and me essential experience. There is an art in reading a script for radio. When we began with 'Navy Mixtures' we were very unsure and amateurish, but the show gave us an opportunity to learn the basics. To my mind its greatest exponents were Tommy Handley, Arthur Askey, Kenneth Horn and later, my sister-in-law Kitty Bluett who worked with Ted Ray.

The first show was recorded at the Aeolian Hall in September 1947 with Jon Pertwee, Claude Dampier, Betty Paul and the Five Smith Brothers. It was an instant success and much of our subsequent popularity was due to little George Inns.

During 'Navy Mixtures' he observed that he hadn't quite brought out our characters properly; but with 'Up The Pole', the two personalities were properly defined. The audience could imagine me as the little man always being bullied by

Ben and the others. I was like the little tramp—the Charlie Chaplin/Buster Keaton character. People felt sorry for me.

Four weeks later, Ben and I put on our first variety bill at the Hippodrome, Wolverhampton. Until then we had been one of two or three headliners but now we were full top-of-the-bill with supporting artistes and getting fifty-five per cent of the net takings. We had recorded 'Up The Pole' on the Sunday and, next morning, I left London at seven for Wolverhampton. When I got there I was nervous, wondering how the advance bookings had gone. The manager looked at me.

'If someone was to give me a hundred pounds,' he said. 'I couldn't buy him a seat for any night of the week. I've even sold standing room.'

I was ecstatic. We were a sell-out at the top of the bill. It was the highlight of our career. I couldn't wait for Ben to arrive. But, as the day wore on, there was no sign of him. Ben always carried the music. He understood music better than I did and he always took the band call. The local orchestra arrived. The other acts turned up one by one and took their band calls but still no sign of Ben. I told the musical director what we were going to do and, fortunately he remembered working with us a year earlier.

'Not to worry,' he said cheerily. 'I'll be in the theatre half an hour before curtain and Ben can hand out the orchestrations then.'

I hung around the theatre all afternoon, pacing the boards and looking down the road, and feeling sick with nerves.

The first show was due to start at ten past six. Still no Ben. We held the curtain till twenty past six and once the opening act had finished, I went on alone to face a packed house.

'I'm very tired,' I said. 'I've been breathing all day...'

Fortunately, there was laughter.

I don't know how I got the words out. I was so nervous that my top lip was sticking to my teeth.

I explained to them that Ben had had trouble with the car. Then came off and started going round the acts asking them to do as long as possible. There was a comedy pianist called Hershel Henlier who was hard to get off if he was doing well. He was due to go on the second half.

'Can you close the first half?' I asked.

He shook his head. 'It takes me half an hour to make up,' he said.

Fortunately we had an illusionist on the bill called Benson Dulay. I asked him to use every trick in the book to pad out the show. Between each act I went on.

I was never a stand-up comic and so I didn't know many gags to tell them. I started talking about my family and the story of Raleano, the strong man. I followed that with the Wakefield lad who wanted to make a eunuch out of me with his clogs. There wasn't much laughter but at least they were interested, so they didn't walk out on me.

I had actually been sick three times between acts when, in the middle of Dulay's performance, Ben walked in.

'Where have you been? What bloody happened?' I screamed.

'Don't ask me where I've been,' he said. 'The bloody car broke down at St. Albans and I've been sitting in a taxi all this time and the bloody driver wouldn't do more than twenty-bloody-five.'

'You should have left earlier,' I said. 'This is our most important week, the first bill of our own for Moss...'

'This is no time to argue,' he said. 'I'm in enough of a state without that...'

He was in a state!

'I haven't time to change into my dinner suit,' he added. 'So, if we're to finish the first act, you'd better get into your lounge suit.'

Suddenly I found myself struggling to get changed while he put on his make-up in a leisurely way and handed the orchestrations to the call-boy. When Benson Dulay finished, Ben casually picked up the off-stage microphone and announced that he had arrived.

The orchestra struck up the music for the song 'Back Again' and we walked on to a rapturous ovation.

'Up The Pole' had done more for us in a month than all the years of working on stage. We had become national names. If a radio series hit, then the artist was made. The radio audience would be curious about what the performer looked like and so they came to the theatres in their thousands. Television has never had that kind of impact. There's no mystery left, nothing to make people leave their homes and visit a theatre. 'Up The Pole' ran for three years and during that time we filled theatres all over the country.

So now we were into the big league as far as money was concerned. One week at the Empire Theatre, Liverpool, we took about four thousand pounds at the ticket office. Our cut was fifty-five per cent. We were paid on the Saturday night in cash; cheques were unheard of in those days. We paid off the rest of the company, about four hundred, and so we were left with close to two thousand. The routine was to pocket the money, and bank it on the Monday after we had done Sunday's 'Up The Pole' show.

Ben took the money and we went to the station and boarded the sleeper. In the morning we got off at Euston and yawned our way down the platform. We were almost at the barrier when Ben stopped.

'Christ,' he said. 'I've left the money under the pillow.'

We looked back. The train was starting to pull out backwards. We ran after it like characters out of a Buster Keaton film, clutching our hats, and jumped on board. Fortunately the cleaners hadn't reached our compartment and the money was still there. Like I've said, Ben never worried about money; but that was the last time he handled the take.

Fifteen

In the spring of 1948, the Hippodrome Blackpool was a sad sight. When Bob Nesbitt and I went to look at it in preparation for the summer season, the old place depressed us. It had been a beautiful little theatre with a horseshoe shaped 'circle' and a small twenty-two-feet-deep stage but the place had fallen into disrepair. It had been used as a cinema and many of the back-stage facilities had been abandoned. There were huge organ pipes at each side of the stage.

Blackie had booked us for the summer season and at first we had turned it down. We had always played the Opera House—the No. 1 theatre—and, besides, we knew the reputation of the impresario, Jack Taylor. If business was good, Taylor was fine. If it wasn't, he made the comics' lives hell. However, Tom Arnold persuaded us to sign. He was going to co-produce the show, so we wouldn't be at Taylor's mercy. We agreed on condition that Bob Nesbitt directed and Joan Davis did the choreography. George Black had drummed into me his first principle; surround yourself with the best in the business and you won't go wrong, and so we stuck out for Bob and Joan before committing ourselves.

But, looking at the theatre, I began to wonder if we had made the right decision. The place was too small to do the big comedy sketches that we had done across the road at the Opera House. Bob and I gazed around the empty theatre, at the great domed roof and the pillars that supported the circle. It was tatty.

'Dear boy,' said Bob, sighing. 'What can we do with this?'

I shook my head. I've never thought of theatres just as bricks and mortar. It may sound corny, but to me they are alive with the sound of laughter and applause. It was criminal that such a place had been allowed to decay.

Bob was a man with a wonderful imagination. Right there and then we began to devise a new concept of doing a show: what if we swagged the domed roof with a velarium, like a circus big top? What if we turned the pillars into palm trees with lighted coconuts at the top? If we took out the organ and the pipes, we could build two rostrums at each side of the stage with the rhythm section on one and the brass section on the other. Maybe we could do away with the orchestra pit and build a run-out up the centre of the aisle with a glass top and coloured lights underneath ...

Why not?

We went back to London and put the idea to Tom Arnold and his partner Jack Taylor. They said it would cost a fortune but Bob Nesbitt sold the idea to them. We called it Coconut Grove. It cost ten thousand pounds to put on (a fortune for a summer show). Later the Hippodrome, London was converted in a similar fashion into what is now the Talk of the Town.

We worked night and day to get the place converted and the show ready on time. Almost until curtain up, we were hard at it. I was in the theatre for thirty-six hours without sleep, helping to get the velarium into position and working with the stage crew. On the morning we were due to open, I was thirty feet above the stage organising a prop that would drop a massive fish onto us in the finale. The grid hadn't been used for years and I was covered in muck. I heard the sound of footsteps on the cat ladder and looked into the astonished face of Jack Taylor.

'What the hell do you think you're doing?' he said.

'Fixing the lines for the fish,' I said.

'But you're the principal comic,' he said. 'You've no right to be up here. We're paying you a lot of money. If anything happens to you, we've got no show.'

He went back down the ladder grumbling and said to the stage manager:

'He's crazy. I've had George Formby, Arthur Askey, Frank

116

Randle work for me but never one like that.' And he went away muttering.

Next, I came down and checked our most important prop—an eighteen-foot pole on which Ben and I were to make our entrance in the show, sliding down it as the orchestra played the signature tune of 'Up The Pole'. It seemed to be okay but, probably because I was tired, I forgot to put on a safety hook to hold the foot-plates down.

That night the house was capacity; the signature tune was played. I slid down the pole with Ben behind me. I stepped off onto the stage and because the safety hook wasn't on, Ben shot straight back up again into the flys. For a second or two I couldn't understand why I was all alone on the stage. The audience were in hysterics. I looked up and there was Ben clinging on. I had to climb back up and help him down. It was a mistake but it started the show off with a bang.

We finished our first spot singing the 'Bells of St. Mary'. I'd had the idea of fixing bells under every other seat in the auditorium: fire alarm bells, telephone bells, all kinds of bells; and as we sang, the bells started ringing. The audience loved it.

Even with all this going on, I was still dozy from lack of sleep. Later in the show, though, I was well and truly woken up! We'd bought a sketch from America called 'Full Fathom Five', in which I go into a shop to buy a pen and the salesman (Ben of course) tells me it will write under water.

'Show me,' was my next comment.

So on comes a perspex tankful of water which I climb into in order to test the pen.

During rehearsals we found that the tank needed three hundred gallons. We tried a hose from the No. 1 dressing room but it was far too slow. Next we opened a fire hydrant. The flow was fast enough but the water was rust-coloured and I wouldn't have been seen by the audience. It took twelve hours of continuous running before we got clear water. The idea had been to heat the water slightly but there had been no time for that. When I went into the tank I thought I would die. I turned blue. After the sketch Ben and the dresser had to rub me with towels in order to get me on for the next spot.

Years later, in fact, the pen sketch nearly killed me. The

original tank had been destroyed and a new one made of two-inch glass. One night at the Pavilion, Rhyl the tank split, the water flowed out into the orchestra pit and fused every light in the theatre. If I hadn't grabbed the edge and hung on, I would have been swept through the glass and cut to pieces.

The Coconut Grove show continued with increasing success. On the first night we ran so long over time that the queue for the second performance was holding up the traffic. The second show, due to start at a quarter to eight did not get under way until an hour later.

We were running so late that we suggested to Jack Taylor that we cut our last spot.

'Not bloody likely,' he said. 'Let the buggers wait. It's like Trafalgar Square on VE Night out there. It's great for publicity.'

It was one in the morning when we went on for the last spot and Ben peered at the audience.

'Do you want to go home?' he asked.

'No!' they roared back.

We didn't get off till half past one. It was one of the best nights of our career.

We had capacity for fifteen weeks and played to seven and a half thousand a week which was fantastic money given that the most expensive seats cost only eight shillings. Charlie Chester was across the road also doing good business and in the afternoons we liked to take a break and play golf. It was idyllic; good money, capacity audiences and golf—the only fly in the ointment was Joseph Locke, a big hard Dubliner who loved a fight. One afternoon, as I went into the dressing room, Ben looked up at me with a rueful expression.

'He had me last night,' he said.

'What are you on about?'

'Joseph Locke,' he said. 'He belted me.'

'What happened?' I sighed. Ben told me that a girlfriend of Donald Peers' had asked him to give her a lift home. Joe Locke walked in and offered her a lift. The girl said no, so Joe belted Ben.

I picked up Ben's table-knife and went to Joe's dressing room. He was sitting at his dressing table putting on his make-up. I stood behind him and looked at him in the mirror.

'Joe,' I said. 'At one time or another you have clouted most people in the show, including the manager. Ben tells me that last night you hit him. Now I'm warning you. If you clout anyone else, I will personally cut your bloody head off.'

I showed him the knife and glared at him, though actually I was terrified. I had no intention of using it and if he had decided to, he could have wiped the floor with me. But he just sat there and looked at me in the mirror.

'You know something,' he said. 'I believe you would too.'

I nodded and left—extremely quickly! But he must have believed me because he was as good as gold after that.

Sixteen

Ben and I didn't go in for self-analysis. We never tried to put our act under the microscope to see what we thought might make people laugh. If we thought something funny, we tried it on the dog. If the audience laughed, then we kept the sketch in and worked on it. Our humour was instinctive. We didn't stop to think about it but we were true English comics. I don't know whether our act would have travelled, but there were some who thought it worthwhile to try.

It would have been interesting to see how the Americans might have taken to us but we were never to find out for sure.

After the Blackpool season, Ben and I decided to take three weeks off and visit New York. It had always been our ambition to see the city and the shows on Broadway. And so, in October 1948 we flew across the Atlantic and checked in at the Gotham Hotel.

We had been there a week when the 'phone rang. It was the William Morris office. Bill Morris, a big New York agent, had, unknown to us, watched the Blackpool show twice and had heard we were in town. He wanted to meet us. He thought we might do well in America and that we should get a spot on the Milton Berle Show.

He also arranged for us to play a theatre in New Jersey as a try-out and so we decided to go there to take a look.

First, though, someone from the agency arranged for us to see Berle at work so along we went to the theatre to watch him rehearse his TV show.

Berle came on like a fighter, wearing a white dressing gown

with his name on the back. There was a guy called Harry Richmond on his show that week and an English impressionist named Florence Desmond. Berle had to get in on each of the acts. That was his style.

I remember watching Richmond sing:
Gee but it's great after being out late
Walking my baby back home.

And Berle came on and said: 'Wait a minute Harry. This is the Milton Berle show. You don't sing it at that tempo. You do it fast. We gotta get some pace in the show.'

It was the same with the impressionist. He was butting into everyone's act. I looked at Ben and we shrugged. It wasn't for us. He would want to be in the 'Timber' routine or whatever. So we didn't do it.

Then we went out to the New Jersey theatre and it was clear that would be a disaster too. It was cine-variety all over again. At the end of the first film the screen was closed off. The orchestra worked on stage and we would have had to work in the band pit which was raised to stage level in between the films. It would have been impossible to do our routine. Still, we stayed for the performance. The place was full of Poles whose notion of audience participation was to fart at the turns. Unsurprisingly, we didn't do the show.

But we did have a good time. We saw all the shows on Broadway and Ben, particularly, had a ball. He was always off on his own. He would get a bird and that would be that. One night I was in bed and the 'phone rang. It was Ben.

'I'm at Bill Miller's Review Club in Washington Heights,' he said. 'There's an act here that's marvellous for Blackpool next year. Come and see it.'

'Ben. It's midnight.'

'That's okay. The last show goes on at half past one. You've got plenty of time.'

Durrant Young, our agent's manager, was sleeping next door. I woke him up and we got a cab. I was wearing a new American raincoat and hat. I looked like Humphrey Bogart in a B movie. We crossed the Washington Bridge and paid the toll. Ben was with a bird and was a bit drunk. We saw the act—which was all right but certainly not worth getting out of bed for. The next thing I knew was that Ben had left. I thought he'd gone to the toilet but in fact he'd scarpered and the waitress presented me with a bill for about seventy dollars. Just as I reached the foyer I saw Ben getting into a cab with a bird.

'That's nice,' I said to Durrant. Then I turned to the commissionaire and asked him to get us a cab.

'That's the last one,' he said. 'You'll have to call one from Manhattan.'

We telephoned and then waited twenty minutes for a cab. We were half way across the bridge when I realised that I had left my Bogart coat in the club. Well, you can't turn round on a bridge. We had to go across, pay the toll and come back. When we got to the club, it was closed. We drove back to Manhattan, paid the toll again and reached the hotel. By this time I'd spent about one-hundred-and-twenty-five dollars. I stumbled up to the room where I discovered Ben in his bed and the bird in mine. So I slept on the settee in the little sitting room, thinking that there were times when it would have been better to have been a single act. . . .

Most men who go to New York return with strange tales about the women there. I was no exception.

I met Phyllis in a club called the Chinese Doll. It was three in the afternoon. Three women were drinking at the bar and they gave us the once-over. One of them sidled up to me. She was blonde I think. She said:

'Hi, my name's Phyllis.'

Then she started talking. Her husband was English, she said. They had been stationed in Newcastle during the war. From there, she went on to tell me her life story, hardly pausing for breath, until six o'clock when we had planned to go to a restaurant.

'I'll come with you,' she said.

'Suit yourself,' I said.

She ate with us, and then we all went to a late night picture.

'I'll come back to your hotel with you,' she said.

'Oh no,' I said. 'Sorry. You can't do that.'

The following morning she 'phoned from the lobby. We were all going out to Coney Island, so she came with us. That night, I got the same routine: 'I'll come back to your hotel.'

'No, Phyllis.' I insisted.

Eventually she went home, to somewhere on Long Island. But not for long.

On the Saturday she was back in the lobby, 'phoning up. She was with us all weekend. We couldn't get rid of her. And every night came the same demand.

'Back to the hotel . . .'

'No.'

But she didn't give up. The last weekend we were there, the 'phone rang again from the lobby. 'Hi,' said the voice. 'This is Phyllis.'

It turned out that she had a deal with her husband. He used to enjoy himself during the week and, at the weekend she would come into Manhattan on her own, on the hunt.

That Sunday night we went out again to a restaurant. At the end of the meal Durrant Young turned to Phyllis and said:

'Why don't you come back to the hotel for a drink?'

I kicked him under the table but it was too late. Phyllis had grabbed her coat. We hadn't been back more than two minutes when he announced that he was going to meet Bob Nesbitt off the 'plane, and disappeared. As soon as he was gone, Phyllis started to take off her bracelets and other jewellery.

'What are you doing Phyllis?' I asked.

She said: 'I'm going to get laid.'

'No you're not.' I replied.

She stopped. 'You son of a bitch,' she said. 'You got me up here under false pretences.'

'You invited yourself,' I said. 'Let me call you a taxi.'

'No taxi,' she said, putting the jewellery on again. 'You're putting me on a train.'

So we got a cab, went down to the station and bought her a ticket. It was three in the morning by now.

'You're coming with me,' she said.

'Pardon?'

'If you don't, I'll scream the place down. I'll say you assaulted me. You're a stranger over here. They'll throw you in the can for ever.'

What could I do? I got in the train with her and schlepped all the way to the middle of Long Island. She stung me for five dollars for her cab fare and by the time I got back to the hotel, it was dawn. Even so, I thought that was the end of Phyllis.

Later that morning the 'phone rang:

'Hi. This is Phyllis. I'm in the lobby.' I chose my next words very carefully.

'Piss off Phyllis.' I said.

And, thank God, she did.

I became very depressed towards the end of that trip. All I wanted to do was to get back to my wife and son. Eventually, we boarded the Queen Elizabeth bound for home and, apart from a brief visit the next year, we did not get involved with American show business again until 1952 when we got an invitation to appear coast-to-coast. The money was good and it was a chance to be seen in America; and so, we set off again to New York.

Ben met the *Daily Express* sports reporter Desmond Hackett on the plane and when we reached New York, they decided to hit a few bars. They went all the way along one side of 42nd Street and back along the other. It took them three days until finally they ran out of money. Ben had to leave his gold lighter with the barman so that he could get back to the hotel and pick up more cash—despite all of which we made it to the rehearsal room in good time.

We were to appear on the Ed Sullivan show with Sammy Davis Junior, Mike Bentine, a juggling act, a fellow called Victor Moor and a Latin American singer called Nino Galvani.

We had all gathered in the rehearsal room when the producer came in. He greeted everyone else, seeming to know them all, then he turned to us.

'Who the hell are you?'

'We're Jewel and Warriss.'

'What d'you do?'

'We're comics, English comics.'

'Shit,' he said. 'English comics. Jesus Christ, how long do you do?'

'We've got a contract that says we've got to do ten minutes,' I said.

'Shit,' he said. 'Ten minutes! Ain't there no television in England? Ten minutes on a TV show is like ten hours. You'll do seven minutes.'

So we went away and cut the act to seven minutes. On the Sunday morning we arrived at the theatre and looked around. We weren't even on the dressing room list. We were sent up the top floor into a place that had once been the wardrobe room.

All day they rehearsed Nino Galvani, pulling him across the stage in a gondola while he sang a Latin American love song. Whenever we asked if we could rehearse the 'Timber' gag, they said, 'Yes, in a minute', but we never got to rehearse. It was chaos.

The show started and we waited our turn. We were closing the bill. Sammy Davis went on and murdered the studio audience. He was outstanding. They wouldn't let him off; he did six minutes over his time; so the stage manager dashed up to our room and asked us to cut another minute from the act. I was sick with nerves. Next came Mike Bentine and Victor Moor. Moor did a long sketch and went two minutes over.

Cut another minute, the stage manager said. According to the schedule, Nino Galvani was to follow the commercial break and then we would close the bill. In the middle of the commercial, however, they decided to scrap Galvani altogether. He went mad. This was supposed to be his comeback but that didn't seem to worry anyone—except Galvani.

'You're on next,' they shouted up to us. By now I had been sick three times. We ran down the stairs and onto the stage as Ed Sullivan announced us:

'Now ladies and gentlemen, straight from London Palladium ... Jewels and Walrus!' As I walked past him, he grabbed my arm. 'Four-and-a-half minutes you bastard,' he said, 'and no more.'

We tried a couple of gags but the audience didn't know what we were talking about. We then went into the 'Timber' routine and died on our feet. We died so badly it wasn't true. Compared to that audience, the Glasgow Empire would have been a comic's paradise. Ben was blazing mad. If he could have got hold of Sullivan I think he would have killed him.

So—that was the Ed Sullivan Show. It taught us a lesson. It also killed any desire we had to work in America.

Jewels and Walrus we may have been in America, but in Britain we had managed to become household names. The late 'forties and the 'fifties were the golden years of the act. We broke records in variety and pantomime and could even afford to turn work down if we didn't like something about it. And even though our American episode had been disastrous, there were some things they wanted from us.

The great American comedians Olsen and Johnston, famous for their 'Hell's A-poppin' show, came over to see what British pantomime was like. They asked Val Parnell where they should go and he directed them to the Palace, Manchester where we were playing in 'Babes In The Wood'. I had resurrected my father's 'Haunted Bed Chamber' sketch from 'Idle-itis'. The original trick scenery had been blitzed in the Second World War when the Salford house was bombed but I'd remade it. After the show Olsen and Johnston took us out to dinner and offered me ten thousand dollars for the sketch but I refused. I didn't want other people working his creation; and they understood my feelings. Indeed, if my son doesn't want it, then the sketch will die with me.

We were playing to packed houses everywhere, drawing audiences because of the success of 'Up The Pole'. That show ran until the end of 1950.

Then, in 1951, we went one stage further when Ronnie Waldman, the head of light entertainment for the BBC, asked us to do a television series. He wanted to do a revue similar to our stage act.

'Where?' I asked.

'Studio E at Lime Grove,' he said.

'How big would the audience be?'

'About two hundred.'

We told him it was difficult. We were essentially music hall comedians and needed a music hall atmosphere. He said it was physically impossible because of the way the cameras operated but I worked out a plan, having seen the way TV shows were done in America. Waldman agreed to it. He said it would be the first time an outside broadcast had been done on such a large scale. He also agreed to allow us to do a warm-up show with the audience on closed-circuit as a sort of dress rehearsal to test out material and to make us less nervous—especially since, in those days, all TV was live. Michael Mills was our director, the script writer was Ronnie Handbury and the musical director was Eric Robinson. We called the show 'Turn It Up' and performed it for TV from the People's Palace in the Mile End Road. We received a letter soon afterwards from Cecil McGivern, programme controller of the BBC, saying that we had begun a new era in television.

At the same time, he suggested that we look for a smaller, more intimate theatre. We found one, Michael Mills and I—the Bedford, Camden Town. It had been empty for years. We went there early one morning and were let in by the caretaker. I found a pilot light on the old switchboard and in its glow, drew a rough plan to show how it might be made into a TV studio. My idea was to take out three rows of seats, then build two rostrums into the audience for the small sets so that we could appear on one of them while the sets were being changed, on the main stage out of camera-shot. Next, we'd build a ramp up the centre aisle for a camera on a dolly with another camera on either side of the auditorium to pick up the smaller sets.

Michael Mills nodded in agreement and that was how it was done. Indeed, when the BBC bought the old Shepherd's Bush Empire and called it the BBC Theatre, they laid it out for television in just such a way.

To do the show we needed zoom lenses but in those days the BBC had only two or three and so we had to wait until the sports programmes were over on a Saturday night and the zoom lenses rushed over to us before we could do the last run-through of the show.

After the third show, Ronnie Waldham walked into the theatre during rehearsals and said to us: 'What does it feel like to have the highest rated light entertainment show on television?'

It felt terrific, that's how it felt. . . .

Pantomime, television, Royal Command Shows, variety; one season followed another. We even did a type of *Folies Bergère* show for Tom Arnold and Emile Littler at the Casino Theatre, London. It was called 'Excitement' and was very spectacular but the audiences could be difficult for comics.

127

Often the theatre was full of foreign tourists, or men who came in for the nudity; they would sit there with newspapers or coats over their knees, staring at the flesh and doing all manner of dreadful things to themselves.

One night Ben and I were doing our cross-talk act when a drunk walked on stage in full evening dress and positioned himself between us.

'I've paid seventeen shillings and sixpence for my seat,' he said pompously, 'And you haven't made me laugh once.' He blinked. 'Make me laugh.'

Ben and I looked at one another and shrugged.

'Well then,' I said. 'If we haven't made you laugh, why don't you have a go. Make us laugh, make the audience laugh.' And we stepped back.

We thought he would be embarrassed and leave but not at all. He simply turned round and, without another word, and aimed a punch at me. I ducked under it, turned him round, got him by the trousers and marched him off towards the prompt corner. He was almost off stage when he managed to struggle free and took another swing. By this time I had had enough. I belted him in the stomach and straightened him up with a right-hander to the chin. As he fell backwards he grabbed my jacket and pulled it over my head.

The audience fell about. They thought it was part of the act. The stage hands grabbed him. I retrieved my jacket and walked back on stage to a round of applause from both the orchestra and audience. We'd lost track of the cross-talk so we finished with a song and dance and left the stage to the sound of cheering.

Our next TV work came in 1954 with a show called 'Double Cross'. I got the idea from the Burgess and MacLean story and presented it to Ronnie Waldman.

'You're not going to like it,' I said.

'Why?'

'Because we have to do a bit of acting.'

'You can do it,' he said. It seems he had more faith in our acting ability than we did; anyway, he bought the idea—a story in which Ben and I played a couple of night club comedians who double as diplomats.

Dick Hills and Sid Green wrote it—a half-hour show every

PALACE
THEATRE
HAYMARKET, NEWCASTLE-ON-TYNE.

6.40 TWICE NIGHTLY 8.50

MONDAY, 21st MAY, 1934
FOR SIX NIGHTS ONLY

National Vaudeville Corporation
PRESENT
A SMASHING HOLIDAY SHOW !

JIMMY JEWEL
AND CO.
IN A DARING EXPERIMENT

CHAS. DUDLEY'S
MIDGET GLADIATORS

THE THREE ROYCES

TERRY | JIMMY JEWEL Jnr.

BEN WARRIS THE TWO MAYFAIRS
BERT MURRAY & JOE CONAN
IN MIRTH AND NONSENSE

BOOK EARLY. Phone: Newcastle 21336.

and Warriss first appeared on the same bill in 1934 – the start of a long and successful

Audiences in Glasgow were notoriously difficult to please. In 1940 Jimmy and Ben played

e: One of Jimmy's rare film appearances was in 1940 in 'Rhythm Serenade'; Vera Lynn lso in the cast.

w: Jimmy is easy enough to spot in this showbiz football team of 1948 standing second from ght. Other familiar faces include Morecambe and Wise, Stanley Matthews, Tommy

'Up the Pole' recorded in 1947-50 was one of Jimmy and Ben's most popular radio

e left: In 1952 Jimmy and Ben appeared at the London Palladium. The 'Timber' sketch agonising to perform but the audiences loved it.

e right: The ice-panto, 'Babes in the Wood' (1955). Jimmy and Ben had to carry a ge of microphone equipment under their colourful costumes.

Over the Christmas of 1955 Jimmy starred in 'Sunday Night at the London Palladium' wi
Bob Hope.

Two of the many faces Jimmy used for an episode of 'The Avengers'.

oy, keen to launch his son Kerry on an acting career, appeared with him in 'Nearest and

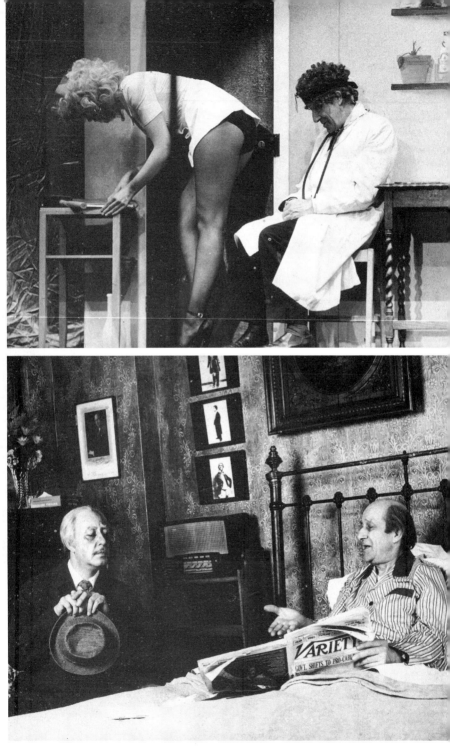

Above: The doctor sketch from Neil Simon's 'The Sunshine Boys' with Isabella Rye.

Friday night from the Shepherd's Bush Empire.

Jill Day played a girl reporter in love with Ben. The poor girl used to come to rehearsals tired out. As well as working with us she was doing the Embassy Club and the Empress, Brixton. One night we were doing the show and the camera was on Ben and me. We were doing a scene in a hotel bedroom and Jill was in the room next door. The camera swung to Jill who picked up a photograph of Ben and began to sing a love song. She was in the middle of the song when we heard a crash. She'd fainted in front of the camera. It swung back to us. The programme, of course, was live.

'The hole in the wall,' I said to Ben.

'What?'

'The hole in the wall routine.'

'Oh yes,' he said, smiling. 'This is a lovely room isn't it?'

'Yes.'

'Supposing you walk over there and bore a hole in the wall ...'

'All right. I'll walk over there and bore a hole in the wall ...'

Meanwhile they were trying to revive Jill. The next scene had the three of us sitting in a car with a back projection of the streets of Paris.

'Why should you go over there and bore a hole in the wall?'

We continued to ad-lib for four or five minutes until we saw the floor manager give us the thumbs up.

'Well, we'd better get in the car then,' said Ben.

'Right.'

So, we got in the car, Jill in the middle with a dirty black mark on her face where she had hit the floor, and the script on her knee because she couldn't remember anything.

It was while doing 'Double Cross' that we realised how tight with cash the BBC could be. There was a scene in Paris where Ben and I were to be met off a train. We were to follow that with a dance sequence with Jill down the Champs Elysée. The BBC wouldn't have it; too expensive; so Ben and I paid for the weekend trip for ourselves, Jill and two writers. Jill added to the bill by leaving her suitcase on the taxi roof and losing it; so that meant a new outfit—a *Paris* outfit—for the lady.

Seventeen

Throughout the 'fifties we continued topping the bill, each season seemingly more successful than the last. We did the lot, even ice-pantomime, learning to skate for the part of the robbers in 'Babes in the Wood' at the Wembley Arena. The audiences were almost ten thousand and it was a tricky business making people laugh when, from the back row of the arena, you looked about three inches tall.

Subtlety didn't come into it. The other skaters mimed their lines which were spoken for them by actors in a control box, but our voices were so well known through radio and television that we felt we had to speak our own lines. We wore special waistcoats under our costumes wired up with twenty pounds of electronic equipment—a transmitter and two batteries linked to a microphone which fastened round our necks and stood out in front of our mouths. And we had aerials sticking through holes in our hats.

It was heavy and unreliable and sometimes it wouldn't work at all—or the mike would produce only two or three words followed by a long period of silence.

One night as Ben and I were skating round the arena, concocting our devilish plan to kill the babes, the system went completely awry. The aerial picked up a local radio cab firm and out of the loudspeakers boomed the message:

'Anyone in the area of Finchley please go to 56 Frognal and pick up a Mr Downing for Euston Station.'

Belle and I were now looking for a baby to adopt. Belle had

130

been told that she could not have more children. The adoption was a long drawn-out process. We tried agencies in London but there were waiting lists. I thought we might try my home town of Sheffield where, or so we were told, we wouldn't have so long to wait. Sheffield for some reason, had a high illegitimacy rate. We took medical tests, got references from Val Parnell and the bank manager, listed prospective earnings and where the child would go to school, and within a year we were told that the agency had a little girl for us. We picked her up while Ben and I were playing the Opera House, Blackpool, with the late Alma Cogan, in 1955. A year later we christened her Piper in the church at Woburn Square in London where Kerry had been christened. It was a wonderful day, made all the more amusing by the fact that the parson was drunk. That evening we held a christening party. I was a happy man. I had a wonderful wife and two children. The next day I was due to go to work at the Britannia Pier, Great Yarmouth. I was being well paid in the job I loved. It was a moment of supreme contentment.

During the party Belle mentioned that she had an appointment next day with an optician. She said that for some time she hadn't been able to see properly out of her right eye. I began to worry. I'm a hypochondriac. If there's anything wrong with me or with anyone I love, I start to get twitchy. I told her not to go to any old optician. I would find a specialist.

I rang Charlie Chester whose brother-in-law was a Harley Street eye specialist and made an appointment for Belle the next day. I was getting ready to go back to Yarmouth when she called and said that she needed an X-ray. She was clearly terrified. I spoke to the specialist and he told me that he suspected that she had a tumour on the pituitary gland. The X-ray confirmed his diagnosis. The tumour was pressing on the optic nerve and could have caused Belle to go blind if it had not been removed quickly. Belle was taken into the London Clinic on Friday for an operation on the Saturday. I hardly slept that week.

Then, as if some awful fate had decided to let me know that happiness is a fragile thing, I received a message to say that my mother had been taken to hospital too.

All of a sudden, everything was falling apart around me. On

the Friday I rang the clinic and talked to Belle as she was having her head shaved. She said she looked like Yul Brynner. I went back to the dressing room and burst into tears. That night, after the second show, I drove back to London and spent Saturday at the clinic. I had booked a small plane from Elstree to take me back to Yarmouth for the first show. Blackie and Durrant Young joined me and we waited all day until the surgeon came out and said that the operation had been a success. The tumour was benign. Again I broke down, this time with relief. I 'phoned Kerry in Yarmouth but when I got through I couldn't speak and Blackie had to give him the news.

The weather was too bad for flying and so Durrant took me to Yarmouth by car while Ben was contacted by 'phone and told to keep the show going until I arrived. I got there half an hour after the curtain had risen.

I was exhausted. I think I'd had only three hours sleep in the week. Next morning the nanny who was looking after the kids for me announced that she was leaving. She already had her bags packed and her taxi ordered. I begged her to stay until I found someone else but she wouldn't. She was adamant. I didn't know what the hell was hitting me. There was only one thing to do. I bundled the kids into the car and took them back with me to London.

First of all I visited my mother in Highgate Hospital. She was grumbling about the place, saying that it reminded her of the workhouse hospitals of her youth. I had her transferred into a private room at a hospital in Hyde Park Corner, then drove to see Belle, leaving Kerry in charge of the baby. Belle was still suffering from the after-effects and couldn't talk to me. The doctor told me that she had been wonderful. The first part of the operation has to be done while the patient is conscious. They apparently freeze the back of the head and bore the holes, and while they were doing the drilling Belle asked the surgeon if they were using a road drill. She really did have the courage of a lion. From the time we found out that she had to go through it, she showed enormous guts and never once let anyone see how scared she was. And the admiration and respect I felt for her then has been with me right through our marriage from that time on.

For the next two week all the kids and I saw was the inside of the car. I took them to the theatre at night then, after the show, drove them to London, spent the night at the flat, visiting my mother and Belle the next day, before driving back to Yarmouth for the night's show. Eventually I found someone to look after them and once Belle and my mother were out of danger I got some rest, only making the return journey three times a week.

Ben and I did a week at Nottingham after the Yarmouth show and we were to go to Taunton after that to appear at the Gaumont Cinema.

Belle came home while we were in Nottingham and on the Saturday night I drove down to see my mother in hospital. She had had another operation. I arrived at two in the morning to find out that she was very ill. I stayed with her on the Sunday, then returned on the Monday morning. I had not been there long when the surgeon told me that she had slipped into a coma. At eleven that morning she died.

I was in a daze. I blamed myself for agreeing to the last operation. I told Belle but she didn't seem to take it in. Since her own operation she seemed to want only to sit and stare into space. I called Ben and told him that he would have to do the show in Taunton without me, as best he could. Once I had made the necessary arrangements at the hospital I started to make my way to Kensington, back to my flat. In the car I realised that they *couldn't* do the show without me. I had all the music in my car! I phoned Blackie who sent Durrant Young to help me to drive the two hundred miles to Taunton. We got there half an hour after the show had started. I did both shows and immediately climbed back into the car with Durrant for the drive to London. I was thinking about the funeral arrangements that I would have to make the next day, when Durrant mumbled: 'Stop the car.'

I looked at him. He was green. All the way back I had to stop for him every few miles. It was something he had eaten. He was sick and had diarrhoea. As I sat in the car watching this great hulk of a man squatting at the roadside, his huge behind lit up by passing head lights, I started to laugh hysterically. I laughed like a lunatic all the way back to London.

It was a terrible time. On the Tuesday night I stayed over in Taunton before going back to London for the funeral. Ben and I had dinner together after the show and during the meal he looked at me.

'Jimmy,' he said, 'I don't think I've been much help to you during all this terrible business but I want you to know that I've nothing but admiration for the way you've kept up your spirits. I wish I had your strength. I'm sure if it had happened to me, I would have collapsed, physically and mentally.'

It was the first time we had been close for a long time and I loved him for what he'd said.

My mother was buried next to my father and when I visit the grave I reflect on their influence on me. Although my father had a most profound effect on my moral outlook and in setting me an example in his love of the family, my mother was no less of a force in my life. She was not a strong woman. Before I was born she had attended a sanitorium with suspected TB and I remember, as a child being aware that she had chest trouble; yet she had no less energy than my father. She not only worked with him on stage, but made the dresses and costumes for his reviews. When we were at home, she cooked all the meals and her Yorkshire puddings and coconut cakes were something to savour. She was a gentle woman who complemented my father in every way.

I remember trying to drive from London to Blackpool to see her in the winter of 1947 when she had been taken to hospital with pneumonia. The roads were blocked and I could get no further than Litchfield. Next day I 'phoned her and she said: 'Oh hello love. I've been worried about you. Say hello from me to your new baby.'

When I told her that I had tried to see her, she said: 'Now then Jim love, you must not worry about me.'

In one of her last letters, she wrote: 'You must have no regrets about me. You've been a wonderful son to me since Daddy died and you have tried to take his place as much as you possibly could.'

I treasure her memory. If I were asked to say which of my parents I loved more, I could make no choice. I adored them both.

Their motto was: 'Be truthful to others, but more important, be truthful to yourself.'

And I've tried . . .

After everything that had happened it seemed that things could only improve, but there was more to come. Belle and I were having physical problems. I went back to see the surgeon. I told him that the sexual side of my marriage had ceased to exist.

He nodded. 'The operation has destroyed the pituitary gland which among other things, promotes the sexual urge.'

'Why didn't you tell me this before?' I asked.

'I thought you'd have known,' he said.

'But I'm just a layman,' I said. 'How could I have known?'

He shrugged.

'So what do I do now?' I asked.

He looked at me. 'You'll have to get yourself a mistress.'

I couldn't believe what I was hearing. I left his office in a daze. And from that day forward I have never had anything to do with another woman. I didn't want anything to put my marriage in jeopardy.

The final blow came around the time that we were playing the Opera House, Blackpool. My niece Betty came to spend the back end of the season with us. Two weeks later an epidemic of Asian 'flu broke out. Betty caught it; she didn't have a chance. She had spent years in hospitals with a tubercular spine and even at the best of times she had trouble breathing. I took her to the hospital and each night after the show I visited her and stayed with her most of the night. One night I helped the nurses. They had been working twelve-hour shifts and getting very little sleep. During that night I saw six people die. I had to comfort a mother whose fifteen-year-old girl had just died. I helped the nurses with the oxygen masks and at the end of the night the ward sister told me to go home and rest. There was nothing more I could do for Betty.

I told Belle that I thought Betty was dying but she was still suffering herself and nothing seemed to sink in. I couldn't sleep and so I went back to the hospital and sat with Betty until it was time to go the theatre.

I was changing in the dressing room when the stage manager came in and told me that the hospital had just rung and that Betty had died. I vaguely remember going through the performance. The cast and stage hands were marvellous. They acted as though nothing had happened. If anyone had offered me pity, I would have broken down. Our final song was 'Side By Side'. I remember singing it in tears but I don't think the audience would have noticed.

Betty was cremated and her ashes placed on my parents' grave in Kilburn. I felt that my last link with the family had gone. I still go to the grave on a Sunday when I am not working and sit awhile. I'm firmly convinced that my father is still around, that he is the link between God and myself, that he is still working on my behalf, helping me in some way. And each night I say three prayers: the Lord's Prayer, followed by a prayer for my family, that they are in good health, then a prayer for my parents, Mona and Betty, that they are leading a happy life wherever they are. I feel very close to them still and I have tried desperately to keep my own family together, to achieve the same family spirit. It is the deepest regret of my life that I have failed to do so.

Eighteen

During the late 'fifties Ben and I did panto each Christmas and a summer season; but we were aware that we weren't the attraction we had once been. Ben and I seemed to be drifting apart and the fire had begun to go out of our performances. The theatres were beginning to close with the coming of commercial television, and at first it seemed that to switch from theatre to television would be our best move.

Lew Grade asked us to appear in a variety programme for his ATV Company—a show called 'Star Time' which was produced by Val Parnell. I told Lew that we had always worked with the BBC but he was insistent. 'Star Time' was a straightforward variety show with a compere linking the acts. We said we would do it only if the show had a distinct theme and if we could use our own writers. He agreed, but said, 'Don't let your agent sting us for money.' The company had been going for only a year and they were still in the red.

So we worked for the same as we got at the BBC—four hundred pounds between us. I collaborated with the writers and we came up with story lines that ran throughout, each sketch linked to the next.

We did the first show in the autumn of 1957, and it felt right. The scripts were good and the show seemed to be working. In those days they went out live which caused some problems. I remember an incident with an actor called Michael Peak, who was so terrified of working with comics that he spent all day, during rehearsal at the Wood Green Empire, sipping gin straight from the bottle. By the time transmission started he was out of his mind. We were doing a burlesque of the film 'Bridge over the River Kwai' and he was playing the part of a Japanese officer. I had a scene with him which involved some dialogue in front of a hut and at the end of the scene he was supposed to look at the bridge through a pair of binoculars. He had forgotten to take them onto the set and so he put his hands to his eyes, made circles with thumbs and forefingers and peered through them.

That was okay, but later I went to fetch him for another scene and I found him in the hut stripped to his underpants with only his tin hat on. He was supposed to march out in full uniform, witness the bridge being blown up, then commit hara-kiri with his sword.

'What are you doing?' I asked.

'I'm going home,' he said, 'I'm finished.'

'No you're not,' I said. 'You've got the hara-kiri scene to do.'

'Have I?' he said. 'Oh dear.'

By that time it was our cue to come out and face the cameras. He came out in his hat and his underpants and looked at the bridge again through his fingers. The camera switched to a model of the bridge which duly exploded, then back to Michael.

'Ah so,' he said. 'The bridge has been destroyed. I commit hara-kiri.'

The problem was that he had forgotten his sword.

Quick as a flash, he turned to a prop palm tree beside him, pulled off one of the leaves and stabbed himself with it.

Just as well it was a burlesque. . . .

Not long after the show was broadcast we were doing a 'Sunday Night at the London Palladium' and Val Parnell walked in. He beckoned us over.

'What does it feel like to be number one?' he said.

The show had gone to the top of the ratings. But within a couple of weeks the director, Bill Lionshaw, told me that Leslie Grade thought that our shows were costing too much. We had special orchestration and extra scenery. I walked down the passage and went straight to Lew.

'Look,' I said. 'You've asked us to take this show over. We're number one in the ratings. Now we hear the budget is to be reduced.'

'Take no notice,' said Lew. 'I'll talk to Leslie.'

He did and we heard no more about it; and although I think Leslie was annoyed that I went over his head to his brother, that didn't prevent him coming to us a little later, when he found himself in spot.

He rang me one Sunday night to say he was in terrible trouble. Michael Holliday who was heading the bill at the Prince of Wales had fallen ill. He had a show, but no headliners.

'I want you and Ben to go in,' he said.

'I'm sorry,' I said. I don't know where Ben is. I think he's in Paris. Besides, we are not variety comics anymore, we're production comics.' What I meant was that we no longer had a twenty to twenty-five minute act to go on with. We would have needed a month to get ready.

'Sorry,' I said. 'Can't help.' Half an hour later Blackie 'phoned. 'You've got to do this to help Leslie out,' he said.

'How did they get hold of you?' I asked.

Blackie was unique in the business in that he wouldn't have a 'phone at home. To reach him, you had to contact a pal of his four doors down and get him to knock Blackie up.

Then I added: 'There's no way we're going to run the risk of being pounced on by the critics for an unprepared act.'

'Where's Ben?'

'Paris, I think.'

He wasn't. He was round the corner; but I didn't know that.

Twenty minutes later Bernard Delfont 'phoned.

'Leslie's in terrible trouble. You've got to help him.'

'Bernard, we haven't got an act.'

At eleven o'clock, Leslie called again.

'Have you found Ben yet?' he persisted.

Eventually I told him that we were rehearsing next morning in Regent Street. If he was still in trouble, he could come and see us. 'I'll see what we can do,' I said. 'But I can't promise anything.'

Sure enough, next morning the 'phone rang. 'What music do you want?' was all Leslie asked. He was so insistent that we had to agree. So we got the 'Star Time' music from the library, joined Leslie at the Prince of Wales theatre, and knocked up a twenty-minute routine.

Blackie was with us and at some point he asked Leslie: 'What are you going to pay them for this?'

'Oh don't talk to me about money now,' Leslie said. 'Let's get tonight's show on and then we'll talk about it.'

So we opened that night. The reviews were okay. They weren't great but they weren't bad either.

Mid-week I call Blackie.

'What's he paying?'

'He wants to give you five hundred pounds for two weeks.'

I couldn't believe it. Our money for a weekly production was, by this time, a thousand.

'Wait a minute,' I said. 'We can walk across the road, open a shop and get five hundred.'

Blackie tried to calm me down. Leslie would make up the rest through the television series, he said. But he didn't. We got the five hundred and not a penny more. At first I decided it wasn't worth getting mad about and put it down to experience. But then we learned that our salary for 'Star Time' was less then other comics were being paid. The fifty-minute show had run off and on for two years. To accommodate it we had not taken a summer season in 1958: the first time we had even missed a summer. Yet we were still on four hundred pounds a show between us while Arthur Askey and Tony Hancock, we discovered, were on as much as eight hundred for half an hour. It seemed additionally annoying because I was helping to create the show, sitting in each week with the writers.

Ben and I decided that it wasn't on.

We were playing the Opera House, Blackpool at the time and we drove down to the Grades' office in Regent Street. Leslie was there. We put our case to him and he listened politely until I made a wrong choice of words. What I meant to say was:

'You need performers as much as performers need you.'

But the gremlins got into my mouth and I came out with:

'You need Jewel and Warriss as much as Jewel and Warriss need you.'

A subtle difference. I could have bitten my tongue. His

expression changed. I could see what he was thinking—that I had over-reached myself, had become big-headed. He gave us the extra money—nine hundred pounds—and four more shows but we didn't work long for him after that. I sometimes feel that incident, with its momentary slip of the tongue, was an important factor in the decline of our popularity.

For some time I had felt that we should change our image and try a domestic comedy series. I worked with a writer called Fred Robinson and dreamed up an idea in which Ben and I ran a corner shop. We sold it to Rediffusion as a thirteen-parter. It did four. It was a disaster. John MacMillan, the head of light entertainment, called us into his office, just as we were about to start rehearsals for the fifth show. At first we thought there was to be a discussion and waited patiently for his comments.

'How do you think the show is going?' he asked at last.

'Well,' I offered, 'It's going to take time to get the characters established but after that, I think it will hit the ratings.'

'We're taking it off,' he said.

He told us that there had been a big shake up of all the commercial companies by the ITA and that three comedy shows were to be axed. There was no room for negotiation. End of discussion; and, as it transpired, the beginning of the end for Jewel and Warriss. We stumbled on for a while after that but our hearts weren't in it. We did summer seasons at Torquay, Rhyl and Morecambe but it was obvious that things would never be the same.

Meanwhile I kept trying to think of new formats for television but my mind was blank. In the end I suggested to Ben that we should have a talk with Blackie. I reckoned that we ought to offer the writers Galton and Simpson a thousand pound retainer to come up with a format for us. They had written 'Steptoe and Son'—a huge success—and I hoped they might find something for us, but neither Ben nor Blackie was interested. They knew that we were reaching the end of the road and I think they were prepared to go down gracefully. By the time the meeting ended, I had realised I'd have to think of something else; something that had less to do with performing than with simply making money.

Occasionally I had wondered how I would make out on the business side of the curtain. The only experience I'd had of finance was through my friend John Galvin. I met John during the war in Olivelli's restaurant. It was a place used by entertainers and we were surprised to see two civil servants there who introduced themselves as John Galvin and Stanley Smith. It transpired that they were no ordinary civil servants. They were the liaison officers between the government and Chiang Kai-shek. I immediately took a liking to them, especially to John. Soon we became firm friends. He would disappear to the Far East for months at a time and turn up without warning. One night he appeared at my door dressed in a pith helmet with a bullet hole in it, a khaki shirt and shorts.

He is the most extraordinary man I have ever met and probably the most brilliant brain I have ever encountered—a true and loyal friend.

In 1952 he was in London to raise finance for a mining and metal company in the Far East.

'How much do you need?' I asked.

'Four million,' he said.

'How on earth can you get an investment of four million?' I was astounded.

'It's easy,' he said. 'You just write down the number four and then add the zeroes.'

He and his partner were thinking of financing TV films for the American market and he wanted me to join him. I didn't take much to the idea at the time. I was a performer first and foremost; but he asked me to think about it.

He said he already had a name for the company—Allied TV Films Ltd, and he wanted me to go to America and check out the market. Such was his persuasiveness that before long he was driving me to the airport!

The trip was not a success. I discovered that the American Federation of Labour did not encourage British TV shows; and even if we had been able to get permission, we would have had to use American musicians for the sound track. I came back and told John who wasn't at all fazed by that. He left instructions that money should be made available for the

142

development of the idea. At that time I decided to remain uninvolved. Now however, with the act in the doldrums, I began to think more and more about business prospects.

I had always been fascinated by projects like Disneyland and when we were playing the Morecambe season, I talked to Bob Battersby the entertainments officer there, together with some local councillors, about an idea I'd had. Then I took out an option on eighty acres of land.

Bob introduced me to a man called Peter Jackson who was building a dolphinarium and a bowling alley in the town. I made some sketches for him and he was impressed. Within a week we had formed a company to build a sort of English Disneyland. We called it Wonderama.

We had plans drawn up and the project was costed at five million pounds. I had the notion that if we could pull it off, Ben and I would have a future: he as publicity and entertainments manager and me as general manager.

It took two years of my life and thousands of letters. The plans were presented to Morecambe council and approved; we applied for planning permission from Sir Keith Joseph and got it; and when things were ready, we hired a suite at the London Hilton to display the scheme to investors.

Dozens of companies turned up; by the end of the second week we had sold one-hundred-and-sixty thousand pounds a year in concessions. Two days later, Labour won the 1964 General Election and all the concessionaires pulled out, afraid to commit themselves. They were worried about how the Labour Party might react to business in general.

That was Wonderama. Dead before birth.

It was a relief however, and a blessing in disguise. I had worked on it solidly for two years and it must have cost me between two and three thousand pounds, but had it succeeded I would have never got back into show business. Belle, for one, was delighted. I think Wonderama would have killed me before long.

The one major compensation, though, was meeting and becoming a close friend of Peter Jackson, another extraordinary man. Years later when I was due to have a fairly minor throat operation, I called him from the hospital and said that the surgeon had told me it was dodgy.

'What did the surgeon say?' asked Peter.

'He said that it was tricky. One slip and I might wake up with no voice and be dumb for the rest of my life.'

'Get dressed,' he said. 'I'm coming to pick you up.'

He took me home and later found me the best throat man in the business who did the job impeccably.

After the Wonderama project collapsed, I still persevered with the notion that Ben and I should continue to work together somehow. I looked at buildings with the idea of turning them into night clubs. I thought that our name still had drawing power and that we could front spectacular shows like those at the Lido in Paris. My idea was for Jewel and Warriss's Diamond Horseshoe; something like that. There was nothing like it in Britain. I even had the dream of a *chain* of Diamond Horseshoes.

Peter Jackson had a bowling alley with a small night club attached in Wythenshaw near Manchester. He was losing money on the bowling club and asked me to work the night club for a while to get it going. I worked there for a month and tried to convince him to close the bowling alley and turn the whole thing into a big night club but he couldn't do it. His company was losing too much money. Eventually Fortes bought it, called it the Golden Garter and turned it into one of the most successful clubs in the north.

Meanwhile Ben and I were working some of the *least* successful clubs in the north. We worked pubs and clubs— terrible bloody places. The whole thing was beginning to fade and fizzle. We couldn't do production sketches in those venues. We did an opening number, a little bit of patter, then a medley, then a routine:

'Everybody loves a baby,' we'd sing. 'That's why I love you . . .'

A girl would come on behind us and start to strip; the audience would applaud and we were supposed to act as though we thought they were applauding us.

We had a projector and a little screen so we could do sketches based on comedy commercials; then we'd be off on some other tangent, say a music routine: 'The Merry Widow' or something of that sort . . .

144

'Ah yes, I knew her. She kept a boarding house in Blackpool—in Acker Street; thirty-five bob all in, with your tea. Married to a Chinaman. Used to bring the tea up sideways.'

Dreadful stuff. All short sharp gags with a laugh in every line. We split the act up and never stayed on too long.

The end came when we were playing the Manchester area. We were being handled by various agents. Blackie had got the needle with us, and rightly I suppose. In any case, he couldn't find work for us and so these others were nibbling at our heels. An agent called Johnny Riscoe had booked us in clubs around Manchester. The first was a pub on the Bolton Road, the next the Tower's Club, Salford, where we dressed in the ladies' toilet. We followed that with the Bolton road pub the following night, doubling at a place called the Mandarin's Club, Levenshulme.

In the pub, I turned to Ben.

'I'm not going to do any more of this,' I said. 'We're not pub and tavern comedians. If we've got to do this, it's time to turn it up.'

Ben nodded.

We drove to the Mandarin's Club with a local agent and we were late. The agent didn't know the way. It was raining stair-rods. There were two heavies on the door, big blokes with flat noses.

'You don't go in there,' one of them said. 'The cabaret's over. You're too late.'

I looked at him and pointed to the agent. 'Argue with *him*,' I said and walked away. I was thinking of the times we'd headlined at Blackpool and the Palladium.

We had another week to play and we refused to do it. We just packed up and went back to London. After that we did a little work, but the rot had set in. Other people were coming up and we'd been around for a long time.

Our final appearance was at the Daily Mail Ideal Home Exhibition in Belfast in 1966. We got five hundred pounds. When we arrived home, I gave Ben his share and he went away. Six days later I got a letter from him.

He wrote that he was buying a restaurant and that he wouldn't accept any more work as Jewel and Warriss; and that was that. I couldn't believe it. He lived just around the corner yet he hadn't come to see me. He hadn't even 'phoned. He had terminated the Jewel and Warriss partnership by letter. I was ill for a week. The letter made me ill, and I still don't understand it. I have never asked him why he did it that way and he has never volunteered a reason.

I have often likened a double act to a marriage. At first, you do everything together. You live in each other's pockets, you even sometimes sleep in the same bed; and like a marriage, there are pressures from outside—there are people around who, sometimes from the best of intentions, want to split you up.

Right from the start there was Hugh Stanhope in Llandudno telling me to stay solo, but I wouldn't have it. And twice Val Parnell tried to influence me that way. After the dress rehearsal for 'Babes in the Wood' at the Palladium in 1950, we came down to the stalls and asked him what he thought.

'It's going to be great,' he said. 'It will be the best pantomime ever put on at the Palladium. We've got all the ingredients. There's your haunted house scene and your trick motor car. Sonny Hale is magic as the Dame. Roy Royston is terrific as the page. We've got your rough and tumble comedy ...' He paused then looked at Ben. 'But really you know, it would be great if you stopped pulling faces and let Jimmy be funny.'

'What do you mean?' said Ben.

'You're mugging all the time while he's trying to get laughs. You're taking the audience's attention away from him. That's not right. You've got to make up your mind one way or the other whether you're the comic or whether he is.'

He was right, but I never paid any attention. It was something that had gone on for years. When we started Ben was simply a straight man, but later we had developed visual comedy like the 'Timber' routine which got laughs for both of us. I understood his frustration. I realized how irritating it must be to always be the straight man and never get any laughs. I knew all this, yet I didn't worry about it.

On the last night of that show when Ben was 'off'—he had broken his foot trying to climb into his house—I went on with the understudy and I never got so many laughs in my life. The understudy was straight. There was no distraction for the audience. Val Parnell and the Grade brothers were there that night and Donald O'Connor, who was to follow us in variety, was in a box.

After the show, my room backstage was packed with people. Val Parnell sent champagne round and Val's wife, Helen, walked in and said: 'You'll have to get rid of that goddam partner. You're such a funny man on your own.'

A few nights later I was having dinner with Donald O'Connor. I nodded hello to Val Parnell who was there with an American impresario called Lou Walters. Val pulled me to one side and said: 'Helen's right. You'll have to do something about this.' But I didn't. I thought there was no way I would do anything to upset Ben.

Then, four years later, Val had another go at me. Ben and I were due to do a show at the Hippodrome but the backer withdrew his money. I met Val at his office and told him.

'I'm glad you're not doing it,' he said.

I looked at him blankly, he was pleased that we weren't going to do one of his presentations.

'I saw you at Finsbury Park and you're not right to come into the West End.'

'What are you talking about?' I said. I was annoyed.

'Ben is working on stage as he is living,' he said. 'He's mixing with all the smart set. He's paying no attention to you on stage. He's gagging. He's mugging. He's talking to the orchestra. He's talking to the people at the side of the stage. It wouldn't be right for you to come into the West End under those conditions. You come in on your own by all means, because there's nothing you can't do. You sing, you dance, you do pathos. You should leave him.'

'No,' I said. 'I can't.'

'I told you in 1950 that you'd got to make a break.'

'There's no way,' I said.

I felt then that we were still a terrific team, still very successful. I felt great loyalty to Ben. Yet Val was so insistent that he gave me the address of a Christian Scientist who, he said, would give me the courage to branch out on my own. Val and his wife were Christian Scientists and they had the special zeal of the newly converted; so I went along to see this character, just to humour Val, who was the sort of man who expected you to do what he asked. He was the biggest wheeler dealer in the business. People went in fear and trembling of him. Anyway, I nodded obediently and went along but I don't remember anything the Christian Scientist said. It was a farce but Val was humoured. I never told Ben about it for many reasons. We had known each other all our lives. It was not just loyalty to someone who had come up the hard way; deep down I loved the man, but I would have been afraid to split with him. I didn't think I had any potential on my own.

The pressure on us to break up wasn't just on one side. Ben left Meggie in 1958 or so and married his third wife Virginia in 1960. That was the start of the real decline. He became secretive and withdrawn. I couldn't talk to him.

And so the partnership ended. In some ways I think we missed out on opportunities. We could have made records like Max Bygraves. We made three films. They were not successful but we could have had a better crack of the whip where movies were concerned. Then there were little things like the comic strip in *Radio Fun* magazine. We didn't get paid for that. It was looked upon as good publicity.

When the end came we were a bit like dinosaurs. We couldn't adapt or alter our image as Morecambe and Wise did. Instead of remaining straight man and comic, they have become two people enjoying what they do together. When we did television, we never possessed the ease that they have. We did the shows live and the physical strain of appearing for fifty minutes every ten days showed in our performance. We were never comfortable.

Yet these are small points. We were lucky and successful—two completely different characters who clicked as a team. Ben is the extrovert; I am the introvert. He loved going to the Ecentric Club and mixing with the pros. I had no interest. All they wanted to talk about was the business. I wanted to get away from it and be with my family. Yet despite—or maybe because of—this difference we got on so well that in thirty-two years we had only one serious stand-up argument.

Ben had turned up late at the Alhambra Theatre, Bradford

in 1963. We were well on the slide by then and I said: 'This is about the seventh time you've done it. I can't take much more of it. It's too nerve racking.'

I suppose I must have sounded like a nagging wife having a go at the errant husband and like in some marriages, the time had come when there was no real communication left. One partner has all the energy, while the other wants to go his or her own way.

I would say to him: 'Give me time and I'll find a vehicle for our age group.' But there was no feed-back, no real enthusiasm. When it started to slip he wanted to get out and do something else. I don't think that he had the great feeling that I had for the act. He wanted to be top of the bill and earn the big money but when it came to the crunch, instead of getting together with me and trying to work out a new image, he was willing to kiss it goodbye. This is no criticism of Ben. I mean it in the nicest way. We were just different. And he was the best straight-man in the business, there's no doubt of that.

Later when I played Willie Clark in 'The Sunshine Boys', I thought of him. It is the story of two comics who worked together for forty-three years and come together for one last show after a break of eleven years. In the play I am asked why we stayed together for so long and I say: 'Why? Because he was terrific. There will never be another one like him. Nobody could tell a joke the way he told it. Nobody could say a line the way he said it. He knew what I was thinking and I knew what he was thinking. One person we were.' Neil Simon could have written that for Ben and me.

So it ended in the summer of 1966 with a letter. Apart from my family, Jewel and Warriss had been my life. I would have fought to the last drop of blood for the name we had established. For two months I was in a state of depression. Then one morning I woke up and thought: 'Christ, I've got to do something. I've got a family to keep.'

Part Three

Nineteen

For a year and a half I made myself ill. I had stomach trouble that was so bad at times that I'd pass out. My doctor sent me to a heart specialist who had me running up and down stairs, but could find nothing wrong with me. Then I had an X-ray of my stomach which showed a shadow.

'Is it an ulcer?' I asked the doctor.

'No. It's in the wrong position.'

'Well, is it cancer then?'

'Could be,' he said. 'I don't think so, but I don't know.'

He told me to come back for tests in six days. The waiting was terrible; bad enough for anyone—terrible for a hypochondriac. Peter Butterworth arrived to cheer me up and every day we walked up and down Holland Park.

'I'll look after the kids if anything happens,' he said.

I went for tests. They put me to sleep and shoved pipes into my stomach. I woke up and stared at the anaesthetist.

'Well?' I said.

'We can't find a bloody thing,' he said.

All this went on for eighteen months and all that time I thought I was going to turn up my toes.

I've always worried about my health. I must have been a pain in the behind to Belle and Ben. My mother would watch me carrying scenery around and say: 'You'll give yourself a heart attack.' The remark stuck in my mind and years later I was so convinced that my heart was going, I managed to give myself palpitations. Four times I went to a specialist and four times he said there was nothing wrong with me; but I

153

wouldn't have it.

'If you're not satisfied,' he said, 'take out an insurance policy.' So I did. The insurance company confirmed that I was completely healthy but it was a long time before I convinced myself.

In addition to being a hypochondriac, I was accident prone which is the worst kind of combination . . . Ever since that first leap through the star trap when I was five I've suffered accidents. I once broke my arm cranking a starting handle. A friend was demonstrating how to swing a rifle around and hit me on the chin with it, knocking me cold. I fell on a suitcase during 'Turn it Up' and hurt my ribs, so the following week I went into the tank for the pen sketch with elastoplast round my chest. As soon as I got in, the bandage shrank so that I could hardly breathe. I got out, ripped it off and tore my skin. I broke three toes on stage at St. Helens, finished the performance and came off to find them sticking up like gravestones. I missed a performance and went on two nights later in plaster. It was the only show I missed. They had to close the theatre because they couldn't get the understudy ready in time, but I made it the next night.

It's the old slogan: the show must go on. My father was the same; most show business people are. Sid James had three heart attacks and went back on; the same with Sid Fields. In any other walk of life if you have 'flu or pneumonia you stay in bed, but not in our business. I remember seeing my mother sit up till three in the morning with pneumonia and a temperature of 103°, sewing stage cloth. And it wasn't like sewing socks. Stage cloth is twenty by thirty feet of canvas painted with black treacle and umber paint. It weighs a ton, yet she was working on it in the middle of the night with a high fever. It's a commitment to the audience I suppose.

On top of my tendency to accidents, I have a problem neck. Now and again the nerves get trapped and I wander around with my head on one side. A friend once recommended a Turkish baths in Castleford as a cure. I had a massage and was sitting half asleep in a cubicle when a man came in and tried it on with me. I hit him from a sitting position and he went out cold. I dressed quickly and ran out, worried that I might have damaged him. I could see the headlines: *Jimmy*

154

Jewel in Turkish Baths Assault. I didn't go back to a Turkish baths after that.

All these accidents were nothing compared to the way I felt during those eighteen months after the act finally broke up, though. I had no real reason to worry. I had been careful never to get behind the eight ball with the tax man. When Ben and I were earning big money we never fiddled, and what the tax man didn't take I put into building societies. In 1963 my accountant advised me to buy property and I bought a block of self-contained flats and a house in Kensington. I was Jimmy Jewel, landlord, and I was busy enough. Whenever one of the flats in the block fell vacant I went in and did it up in order to let it as a furnished place. I did the carpentry and the painting and decorating. There was enough to be done.

At the same time I was trying to get Kerry started in the business. He'd shown no interest until one year, when Ben and I were playing Blackpool, he decided he wanted to learn to play the drums. The local drummer from the theatre orchestra taught him. Once he'd decided he wanted to get into the business, I thought he should form a group. We got a pianist and a guitarist and they called themselves the Kerry Jewel Three–-playing standards and Beatles' songs; but they could never agree and they didn't rehearse enough. They were always breaking their equipment. I got them a season at Butlin's in Bognor but they didn't have enough material and after two weeks they lost their voices. I had to get someone to go down and sing for them.

It was a flop and an expensive flop; with guitars, amplifiers, microphones and suits, the whole operation cost me about four thousand quid. I wasn't very pleased.

After that he decided he wanted to be a comic. He thought it would be easy. He played clubs where he went on and came almost straight off again; the managers would say: 'You're no bloody good. Here's the money. Go home.' It broke his heart but when he realised that it wasn't going to be easy, he began to work at it. Now, in Australia where he lives, he can do a forty-five minute spot and has become a good raconteur.

During this period I suppose I had pretty much settled for retirement from the business—despite the fact that I was only in my mid-fifties. Ben and I had had great success. We had travelled the world and earned good money. What more could anyone want? But even as I asked myself that question, I knew that I wasn't content simply to fade away.

One night I was watching TV—a BBC documentary about two guys who lived in the same street. One was Catholic, the other Protestant. One supported Liverpool, the other Everton. They were great mates until the teams played each other, then whoever lost would get his kids to break the other guy's windows and put tar on his outside lavatory seat, or soot through the letter-box.

I thought: what a smashing idea for a comedy series. I rang up George Inns and told him about it. I even had a title: 'Side by Side'. George thought it was a good idea and together we went to the BBC and saw Frank Muir who was Head of Comedy.

He liked the idea. He wondered who might write it, then answered the question himself. He had two friends called Vince Powell and Harry Driver. Could they do it, he asked.

I said: 'Sure, give it to anyone you want.' Then I left.

When I'd gone, Frank turned to George and said that he thought it was a good idea for Jewell and Warriss.

'No' said George, 'they're not working together any more.' It was just an idea for someone else, he pointed out. If there was anything to come out of it, a few quid for Jimmy say, then fine.

'Oh,' said Frank. 'I thought he intended it for them.'

When I got home, Belle told me that Frank had 'phoned to suggest I do a play for him. I thought he must have been talking about 'Side by Side'.

I rang him back and he told me he had a comedy play called 'Spanner in the Works' with Norman Rossington playing a foundry manager. He wented me to play the militant shop steward.

'It's not for me, Frank,' I said. 'I'm not an actor. Thanks very much, though.'

'Well, I think you can do it,' he said; and he sent me the script. It was good. After I read it I thought, well . . . maybe.

I asked Belle and Kerry and they both said the same thing: 'What have you got to lose?'

So I did it. I was scared, dead scared because I never

thought I could act, never thought I had any chance working on my own.

At first the omens weren't too good. The director, a man in his forties, came to see me and said that he was too young to remember Jewel and Warriss; then he took me round the studio and pointed out the cameras as if I had never seen one before; and later I learned that Vince Powell and Harry Driver didn't want me at first. They had been a double act themselves and they didn't think a comic could do it.

When I started rehearsals, they must have been anxious because I was tending to go over the top. There was no audience to react to and my facial expressions were too exaggerated. Once the director explained, though, I began to get the hang of it. Norman Rossington was a great help to me but I was very nervous when the show was eventually transmitted. I don't like watching myself on television at the best of times and I could hardly bear to look. But once the show had finished, the 'phone never stopped ringing. Everyone who called had something nice to say. It had worked; and I owed the success to Frank Muir for his faith in me.

A week or so later I was offered the part of a comic turned bingo-caller in a fifty minute play called 'Lucky for Some'; and as soon as I began to realise that I was back in show business—that people were offering me work again—all my symptoms of illness vanished. Magically I was well again.

'Lucky for Some' was followed by an episode of the 'Avengers' in which I played a homicidal clown who kills people because he objects to the variety theatres being closed down. I enjoyed that part! Then I got a call to see Peter Eckersley at Granada who had seen 'Lucky for Some' and wanted to pair me up with Hylda Baker in a series to be written by Vince Powell and Harry Driver. Hylda would play Nellie Pledge, the owner of a pickle factory; I was Eli, her brother.

The pilot show was a great success and the producer was keen to go ahead with another thirteen. From the word go, I could see that things were not going to run smoothly and for that reason I would have preferred to opt out: but they talked me into it. I couldn't pretend that my four-year association with the show was a happy one, but there would be no point in raking over all the details now—it's in the past. Suffice it to say that Hylda and I didn't enjoy the happiest of working relationships. The concept finally ran to four series and a film, so it's plain that the difficulties can't have been transmitted to the audience.

After that I worked on a smashing show called 'Spring and Autumn', with a kid called Charlie Hawkins—sheer pleasure. It was after the first few programmes in the series, that Vince Powell called me up and made a lunch date. He said that someone from Thames TV at Shepperton wanted to see me.

'Fine,' I said.

'We'll take my car,' he said.

'Fine.'

'I'll take you to lunch first at the *Trattoo*.'

'Fine.'

Fifteen minutes later he rang back.

'I think we'll take your car.'

'Okay. We'll take my car.' What does it matter whose car we take, I thought. Then he rang back again.

'Make it twelve thirty.'

'Fine.'

I thought: he's going barmy.

My wife and daughter had been acting oddly too. A couple of nights before the lunch, Belle said that she was going out to a fashion show. She never went to fashion shows; in fact she never went anywhere without me. Piper went out that night as well, saying she was going to dinner with someone, and left me on my own.

Even more oddly, they came back together.

'We met in the lift,' said Belle.

'Oh yes,' I said.

Something strange was a-foot. Whenever the 'phone went Belle would dash over and pick it up.

'Who was it?' I'd ask.

'Oh, some Indian who got the wrong number.'

Vince turned up at twelve on the appointed day to take me to lunch. All through the meal he kept looking at his watch and slinging back the brandies. Eventually we drove out to the TV studios. When we arrived, a gateman stopped us.

'Mr Jewel,' he said. 'Mr Philip Jones has reserved a parking place for you.' He told me to reverse into the space and as I backed in, a little Volkswagen behind me blew up. The bonnet flew upwards with a bang.

'The bloody IRA are here,' I said to Vince. I got out of the car and there was Eamonn Andrews getting out of the Volkswagen with a broad grin on his face and the famous red book in his hand.

'Jimmy Jewel, actor, comedian,' he said. 'This is your life.'

'No way,' I said and backed off. I'd always maintained that if anything like that happened, I would walk away from it, principally because I didn't consider myself all that important. I thought that the show should be about people who had done something for the good of mankind. But I looked at his face and at Vince's. They were grinning at me and a thousand thoughts flashed through my mind. They might have flown my sister-in-law in from Australia. (They had.) They might have brought Ben Lyon in from California. (They hadn't.) I couldn't back out and disappoint everyone. So I went along with the whole thing; and in fact it was a marvellous night.

It was just as well though that they didn't have my car wired for sound or the audience would have had an earful. Later I found out that the producer had hired an actor to play the parking attendant. The original idea was for the guy to get into an argument with me but Kerry put the blocks on that idea.

'If you do that,' he said, 'the old man will probably give him a right-hander.'

Ben came on and nearly took the show over. Then there was Tessie O'Shea, Jon Pertwee, Betty Paul, four of the Five Smith Brothers, and the family of course. I felt very emotional about the things people were saying. It was as well I wasn't asked to speak because I wouldn't have been able...

My only regret is that the programme was done too soon—'This is Your Life'—it sounds almost like an epitaph. I wish they had waited until now. Because it was after the programme that I began to work as a serious actor.

159

Twenty

One morning in the summer of 1973, the 'phone rang. It was Bernard Delfont's office. I was told that the production manager, Richard Mills, had something for me, so I went to see him.

'We've got a play by Neil Simon,' he said.

I knew the name and that he had written 'The Odd Couple', but that was about all I knew. Mills told me the story of 'The Sunshine Boys'.

'We'd like you to do it,' he said, 'and we want you to work with Ben again.'

I suppose it seemed an obvious idea to him but I didn't fancy it. I was established on my own now and I thought it would be a mistake to go back; and I knew that the public has a short memory. He was persuasive though and it is a marvellous play, so I agreed.

I wondered what it would be like, working with Ben again but he quickly answered that question. He didn't want to do it. He told Richard Mills that he had a steady job and didn't want to risk something that might or might not run. So they searched around for someone else and eventually came up with Clive Dunn. Would we go to New York and read for Neil Simon. 'Sure thing,' we said; 'why not?'

I boned up on the play, working with my tape-recorder to prepare for the reading. Clive and I flew to New York in October. We were staying at the Algonquin. The producer, Alexander Cohen, had ordered a welcome for us—in our rooms was a basket of fruit and two envelopes containing fifty dollars spending money a-piece. I thought: 'That's nice.' I didn't exactly need the money; in fact I had a bank account in New York; but clearly he meant well.

We met Cohen for brunch, saw the matinée that afternoon, and read for Neil Simon the next day. When we had finished he complimented me on my timing. 'It's amazing,' he said. 'All you people who've been in vaudeville turn out to be marvellous actors.'

I didn't disagree with him. What I did say, though, was that if he wanted me to play, I would need to know soon so I could rearrange the second 'Spring and Autumn' series. Later that afternoon, Clive and I went to Cohen's office, on the top floor of a Broadway theatre.

He didn't beat about the bush. Neil Simon wanted me but he thought that Clive was too young for the part. Clive took the next flight home but I stayed on to watch the show a couple more times before returning to England, where I waited to hear what my next move should be. First the TV series was put back; then I turned down a Palladium panto because I was expecting the call from New York. Finally Richard Mills rang and said: 'We're not going to do it. Simon won't accept any of our nominees for the other part and we're tired of sending people over there.'

'Well, if you're not going to do it,' I asked, 'can I?'

'Talk to Cohen,' said Richard. 'They've got the rights.'

I rang Cohen and put the proposition to him.

'Sure,' he said. 'Neil was knocked out with you. I'll ring him.'

A little later he called back. 'You've got the rights,' he said.

Now I had to find the money. I rang Peter Jackson.

'What do you know Peter,' I said. 'I've got the rights for 'The Sunshine Boys'.'

'What's it going to cost?' he asked.

'About twenty thousand.'

'Okay,' he said, 'put me down for half.'

Then I went round to Blackie's office and told him about it. As we were talking, a business friend of Blackie's named Phil Hindin walked in, listened to the conversation and said he wanted to be in on it. Next, Helen Arnold, Tom's widow, decided she wanted a piece. And so we were all set to go.

I asked Alfred Marks to play opposite me and he agreed. Neil Simon was happy with Alfred, but he kept turning down directors. Eventually he accepted Patrick Garland.

'I'd love to do the play,' said Garland. 'But I'd like to re-write it and anglicise it.' 'No way,' said Neil Simon. Exit Garland.

So, by now we had the cast—and the Picadilly Theatre was booked, but we lacked director. I called Neil Simon.

'You'll have to let me choose my own director,' I said.

'No,' he said. 'I won't do that.' He thought about the situation for a moment, than said, 'Look, you have a contract with me that calls for first-class air fare and hotel accommo-dation for the rehearsals. I'll scrub that condition. You take my brother Danny, give him the same deal that you were going to give Garland and let him do it. He knows the play.'

And that's what we did. The play opened in April 1975 to the best notices I've read in my life. It was fantastic; but even so, we were aware that we had the wrong theatre. No-one passes the Piccadilly. If it had been at Wyndham's or on the Avenue—Shaftesbury Avenue that is—we'd have run for ages. It cost us four thousand a week—fifteen hundred rental and two thousand-five hundred in overheads—and it ran for twelve weeks. I lost about three thousand pounds but I don't regret it. It was a marvellous experience.

During the negotiations for 'The Sunshine Boys', I had been asked to read a script called 'Comedians' by Trevor Griffiths—the story of an ageing comic who teaches his craft to a group of young men at evening class. I read it three times then invited Trevor and the director, Richard Eyre, to my flat.

'It's a marvellous play,' I said. 'But I don't want to do it.'

They looked at me in surprise.

'In the first act,' I said, 'every other word is a four-letter one and I don't want to be associated with that.'

They looked at me as if I were some sort of old-fashioned moralist.

'I know I'm not a writer,' I said. 'But I know when one thing kills off another. In the second act a boy tells a gag about a feller running out of a building stark naked and a copper asks "Where's the fire?" He says, "Never mind about the fire. If you see a naked bird running down the street, f*** her,

162

she's paid for . . ." Now, if you use that sort of language in the *first* act, the boy has nowhere to go with that gag. You've already lost the shock value.

'It's like a comic act—if you can't get laughs with good material, don't fall back on blue stuff. And you can't follow a blue comic either. If you come on after that sort of an act, you've had it. It's the same thing.'

We talked about it for two hours and eventually Trevor agreed, somewhat reluctantly, to take out a lot of the bad language in the first act; so I agreed to do it.

Then, as rehearsal time approached, I got cold feet. I didn't think I could succeed. It was such a big, dramatic part. I didn't think I had the experience.

Then I thought back to something Trevor had said: '*You're* the one we want,' and I told myself 'If they think I can do it, I must be able to.' So I quashed my misgivings and drove to Nottingham where rehearsals were due to begin. I was an hour and a half late and the atmosphere was a bit hostile. I could sense that the young actors were thinking: 'Who is this comic walking in here late? He's never done a straight play before.'

But I soon won them over, thanks, in part, to the nature of the play. They began to come to me, singly, and say: 'How about this gag? Should I pause here or run it through?' I think I became a sort of father figure to them.

On the opening night I became quite emotional. There is a speech towards the end where a character talks about hatred. I had to say: 'How old are you? Twenty-four? Twenty-five? What do you know about hate? Before you were born I was in Germany doing an ENSA tour and we went to Buchen-wald . . .'

As I was saying this, I thought of that terrible night in the hospital when all those people died of 'flu. I don't know what made me think of it, but suddenly it was very real. I broke up and started to cry. It was completely wrong for the part and at the finish Richard came backstage and asked what the hell was going on. I apologised of course, but I'm not sure he understood.

'Comedians' ran for four weeks in March 1975, after which I did 'The Sunshine Boys', then back to 'Comedians' at the

Old Vic in October. The play was held up so that I could finish my run in 'The Sunshine Boys'. Richard Eyre told the producers that they wouldn't put it on in the West End until I was free, which made me feel very proud.

On the opening night we were given a standing ovation. There were all manner of people out front that night—Angela Lansbury, Frank Finlay and Olivier I think. It was then that I realised I had a future as a straight actor.

The play transferred to Wyndham's and ran for six months. On the Wednesday of the last week I did something to a disc at the bottom of my spine. I went to a physiotherapist who pulled it around and made it a bloody sight worse. A doctor gave me some injections of cortisone and I worked the Wednesday and Thursday shows. By the Friday the pain had moved to my hip so I called the doctor again.

'I don't want to know,' he said. 'Go to bed.'

'But I've got to work tonight,' I insisted.

'Suit yourself,' he said. 'But I'm not giving you any more shots.'

I couldn't work that night in fact, and the understudy came on, but I managed to crawl on for the final performance on the Saturday. It was a very emotional night. In the last scene, all the young comics drift off stage one by one. On this occasion they all behaved strangely as they left: hanging back as if they didn't want the play to end. Finally I was left with the last character—played by an actor called Dave Hill. He had to give me a pipe—something that (in the story) they had whipped-round to buy for me. When he gave me the pipe, he was in tears. That set me off and the whole final confrontation between us—a twenty-minute scene—was played in tears. It was magic. It worked. And when we came back to take the call the entire cast was in tears. We took thirteen calls then I went away and locked myself in my dressing room for half an hour to get over it.

So there I was at sixty-six, a former little red devil, dung-covered acrobat, juvenile lead, sketch comic and now legitimate actor. If I'd ever stopped to think about it, I might have realised that there was a tradition of variety comics turning to the straight theatre. Sid Field, had he lived, would have been one of our best actors, I have no doubt about that. Alfred

Marks and Max Wall, too, are both well-respected actors. Probably all variety comics are frustrated actors just as, so they say, actors are frustrated comics.

At first, when I went 'legit', I wondered whether I might encounter snobbery or animosity among actors or directors, but there was only one occasion when this happened. I was working on a TV play called 'Greenhill Pals', about a bunch of Old Contemptibles who take a trip back to the war graves in Belgium. The director, Gordon Fleming, had it in for me. He kept telling me that I was pulling faces in front of the camera. Eventually I got fed up with him.

'If you don't leave me alone,' I said, 'I'll give you a bloody right hander.'

That was the only occasion, though. No-one else ever got snooty about working with a comic. Why should they? As Dickie Henderson once said: 'A dramatic actor is a comedian who isn't getting laughs.'

Twenty-one

One autumn morning in 1977, Sam Kirkwood, who was secretary of the Variety Club of Great Britain, rang me.

'We'd like to give you a lunch,' he said.

'Why?' I said. 'What the hell have I done?'

'Well, you've worked a lot of Variety, supported a lot of our charities. You're a member of Variety and we feel we owe it to you. So, who would you like to come?'

I named a few people from the past and present and put the 'phone down. Again I was terrified. I'd been to a few of these lunches. The guest always makes the last speech, after five or six others have been on either eulogising him or cracking snide gags. With me, the old joke applies: some people have lunch and up comes a speech. I make a speech and up comes the lunch.

The event was held at the Savoy and filmed by Thames TV. Jon Pertwee made the first speech, then Dickie Henderson, Alfred Marks, Ben, and Tom O'Connor. Ben was great. He didn't try to be funny. He was nostalgic and emotional.

But of all the speakers, Ted Ray stood out. I was so happy to see him because he had been involved in a terrible car crash earlier in the year. I had visited him in hospital and he was in a very depressed state. The first time I saw him he kept going on about being a bloody idiot. He felt guilty because he'd had a couple of drinks and taken some pills or something and he had nearly killed someone other than himself. He thought he might never walk again. All I could do was sit and listen and I think I helped to bring him out of his depression.

So when he got up to make his speech I was delighted. He was marvellous—enormously funny. He attacked the audience as if he were playing the Empire, Glasgow—second house. When he finished I got up. I'd rehearsed a speech but I didn't think that I could top Ted's. I wound up giving, instead of the planned address, a very emotional speech about what my life in show-business meant to me. I paid compliments to all around, to everyone who had helped Ben and me on our way.

My only regret was that Blackie had refused the invitation. We had had a parting of the ways a few years earlier when I realised that he couldn't represent me as a straight actor and he never forgave me.

As things turned out, that lunch was the last appearance Ted Ray made. Ten days later he died.

By this time I was becoming involved in 'Funny Man'—a series based on my family and our life in the theatre. When I'd played in 'Greenhill Pals' the writer, Brian Thompson, listened to some my stories and said that they should become a book or a TV series. I wrote out a one-and-half-page synopsis and made a date to have lunch with Verity Lambert who was Head of Drama at Thames Television. She read it as we went into the restaurant and before we had even sat down, she said that she wanted to do it. It was to be a series about a travelling company in the 'twenties and 'thirties. I wanted to show a true picture of show business in those days; not a schmaltzy American-type backstage musical, but the real thing.

I sat down with Brian and we worked out a synopsis for a thirteen-part series. I hoped that he would write the lot but he was commissioned to do only the first two. That was a bit of a blow to me: I felt that the series needed the kind of consistency that a single writer could provide. I said that I would need to work with whoever else they brought in. No, it's okay, I was told: Brian will work with the other writers.

Brian wrote the first two scripts and we met the two producers and Verity Lambert at Thames. During the meeting, Jeremy Isaacs, who was Programme Controller, came in and thanked Brian for two marvellous scripts. Three weeks later Brian was sacked. He had nothing more to do with the series and I was never asked to meet the new writers. The whole thing was taken out of my hands. A number of things I wanted to put in never made it. I was told that the director knew more about drama than I did and he didn't want me to see the scripts until they were done. By this time Verity had left Thames for Euston Films and there was no-one to whom I could appeal. I felt that she would have understood my concern, since apart from being one of the best brains in the business, Verity is a hell of a nice person.

We started recording in October 1978 then went to the New Tyne Theatre, Newcastle to play those scenes that took place in a theatre. But at the end of the second week, a strike closed it and we had to return to the studios. When we finally got back to Newcastle it was January and the coldest winter I've ever known. The buses in the city didn't move for two days and the theatre was freezing. It was still in the process of being re-built. There were gaping holes in the walls and no central heating. Still, we eventually finished the theatre scenes and travelled back to the studio and then to the Wimbledon Theatre. I was just about to do the big, final scene with Pamela Stephenson when the director suddenly yelled, 'Everybody out'. It was another strike and held up the show for five months, putting it out of the scheduling slot for the following season. I had written the synopsis in September 1976; the show didn't finally go out until April 1981.

To my mind, the members of the family in the series were too aggressive with one another and the incidents too dramatically-forced. It wasn't like that at all. I wanted to show the comic side of it, the daft things that happened. There was to be a scene that demonstrated the hard work involved in getting the show from one town to another, but that was never filmed. I thought the series lacked balance and I was sorely disappointed in it.

One of the great sadnesses in my life is that there are no more theatres; and it seems clear to me that commercial television has ruined the theatre. Those who pioneered commercial TV had huge vested interests in Moss Empires, yet none of them seemed to care about the theatres one way or another. They were sold off as quickly as possible and office blocks put up in their place. Commercial television began in

1955 and within ten years, the Empire, Edinburgh, the Empire, Glasgow and the Empire, Sheffield, all ceased to exist.

Now there are only the clubs—and you can't do sketches or productions in the clubs. There isn't the room to put a set on stage or to fit up proper lighting; and because the audience is eating and drinking, the haven't the concentration for a sketch—they don't want three- or four-handed dialogue, just straight-forward jokes from stand-up computer gag men. An era has passed; it won't return.

Most of the comedians who appear in television situation comedy are not properly prepared. There are some who have a natural knack for it but most of the sit-coms seem to lack new ideas.

Twenty-five years ago every town boasted at least two theatres. There was Variety, with eight or nine acts on the bill. Now you couldn't fill four theatres in the whole country with Variety acts. Some might say that people don't want to see that sort of theatre but this notion has been disproved by people like Ian Watt Smith who has taken over the Churchill Theatre, Bromley which plays to eighty per cent business by being multi-purpose. It stages Variety, good plays, children's theatre. He has introduced a subscription scheme and attracted five thousand members as well as persuading all sorts of people to sponsor shows.

The same applies to the Theatre Royal, Nottingham which cost two million pounds to refurbish but which now rarely has empty seats. With a little ingenuity it can be done, but the moguls, the big impresarios who live in London, are not interested in the provincial theatre. There are a few independents with vision and enthusiasm—men like Michael Codron and Duncan Welden—but there aren't the theatres left for them to put shows into. And who is likely to spend a minimum of two million to build a new Empire Glasgow? Indeed, why should the ratepayer or the Arts Council have to subsidise the theatre when the television people are making vast profits?

They are complacent even about their own output. They think: 'Why spend money on situation comedies when quiz shows, that are cheap to make, can usually achieve a top ten rating?' It's all very short-sighted. If we're not careful, our television shows will be indistinguishable from those in America.

I made one attempt to fight a rearguard action, but it ended in disillusionment. In 1978 I heard that the old Lyceum, Sheffield was running Bingo. I had played there many times, so when two boys from a group called the Friends of the Lyceum came to see me I agreed to go with them to talk to the town clerk and several of the local town councillors.

We met at the Town Hall and talked about ways in which we might re-open the theatre. The owner wanted eighty thousand pounds for it and another forty or fifty thousand would be needed to refurbish it. I went away and came back with a plan which would enable us to keep it open all year round. I suggested that the council should buy it. Then I would take it on at a peppercorn rent for a fixed number of years. There would be a ten-week pantomime season, then from February to May we would put in the Royal Ballet, the big opera companies, six weeks of amateur productions and two weeks' variety. From the middle of May until the middle of September the theatre would be prefabricated like Coconut Grove and there would be lavish productions with an ice floor and a watershow. In September it would become a legitimate theatre again, with opera and plays until the pantomime season.

The councillors didn't want to know. They had no vision. To begin with they didn't like the idea of turning the place into a night club in the summer. They turned the plan down flat. So a few months later, the Friends organised a charity show to raise money for the theatre. We had an excellent bill. Acts came from all over the country. It was to go on at the Civic Hall on a Sunday night and it was a sell-out. Then, three days before the show, the boys rang me to say that the council had been on to them to point out that there could be no comedy. Because it was a Sunday, no jokes were allowed. If anyone told a joke, then the theatre would be closed. We had to cancel Alfred Marks and several other comedians. As for me—I could only compere. But we did it. Among the packed audience were police officers ready to pounce if anyone so much as chuckled.

Even though we'd had to cancel the comics we still had a

large bill and were over-running. The manager came back-stage and told me that if we didn't stop by ten he would pull the plugs. When the deadline came, we still had four acts to go on. I went out and apologised to the audience and explained the situation. As far as I was concerned, the show had been virtually sabotaged. I was furious. I wrote to the *Sheffield Telegraph* when I got back to London saying that, although I loved the city, I wouldn't be back.

I did go back eventually though—in 1980 to do a radio show for the BBC and to talk about my early days. I visited Cobden View Road and then went to the Lyceum. It is standing only because it is a listed building but I was looking at a wreck. The circle ceilings had collapsed and there were gaping holes in the roof and walls. Rats scuttled everywhere. It was like a horror story. It seems sinful to allow such a place to fall to pieces; I came away from Sheffield feeling terribly depressed.

Twenty-two

Playing in 'Comedians' and 'The Sunshine Boys' gave my life an added dimension: something I didn't have as a comic. I could say things on stage, the Buchenwald speech for example, that I felt to be important. Someone else had written the words and I had learnt them. Although I can think things out like the idea for 'Funny Man', I find it difficult to put emotion into words. In a way I am more relaxed on stage than in real life; it's the Pagliacci thing. Maybe I hide behind whatever character I play. I don't know.

I get very emotionally involved with people but I find it difficult to express my feelings. I even find it hard to talk to my son face to face. I try setting it down in long letters but even that doesn't seem to work. When I write to him about the things that involve the family, he makes no mention of them when he writes back. I can't seem to make him understand how much he and the family mean to me, and how much I wanted the same relationship with him as I had with my father. Perhaps I am asking for too much.

In March 1978 Kerry took his family with him to find a new life in Australia. I pleaded with him not to go but he wouldn't listen. He had been getting work here—a pantomime, club work, a season as principal comic in Lowestoft—but he was depressed about not being able to break into television. For him there was an additional difficulty—that of simply being my son. Like other sons of show-biz fathers—Tony Bygraves for example—he was unfairly criticised, despite the fact that he has a lot of talent. The problem was that by the time Kerry decided he wanted to be a performer, Ben and I were splitting up. If we had been running revues, he might have progressed into them in the same way as I did with my father. The timing was wrong, I suppose.

A number of people tried to talk him out of going abroad. He had no trade, no contract, only the name of a relative who worked in television. I was heartbroken. I was also worried, because I was due to go into hospital for a throat operation and I didn't know what they would find when they opened me up. What if I was seriously ill? Who would look after Belle?

Right up to the last I hoped he wouldn't go. Both Peter Jackson and Vince Powell attempted to persuade him to stay. Sir John Galvin, who was passing through Heathrow, tried to talk him out of it three minutes before the flight was called. But he went; and, in fact, has done quite well out there. He'll never come back. He has told me that.

I miss Kerry and our grandchildren very much. I have always believed that when children are grown and married, they should lead their own lives and, unless they go out of their way to ask their parents for advice, then the parents should not interfere. I would never want to live with my children and be a burden to them but when I get too old to work, it would be wonderful to know they are not far away.

I really care very deeply for all my family and for very close friends and it is doubly difficult for me to comment about our adopted daughter, Piper. Our relationship with her began to be fraught when she was about eight and as time went on, things became worse and worse. Often I've sat with her and talked to her for hours to find out what's gone wrong, but without success. All I know is that it is a great sadness to Belle and to me. We would be so very happy if she were to come home to us and be our daughter again.

I still see Ben now and again. His restaurant didn't work and he sold it. Then he did some work for Bernie Delfont in Old Time Music Hall at the Winter Gardens, Blackpool where he met a man called Bourne who ran a caravan park with an on-site entertainments club at Fleetwood. Ben worked for him for a while as entertainments officer. He booked the acts and got the club going but he didn't have a contract. On the day he came to London for 'This Is Your Life', he was covering up a shock. The previous day Bourne had walked into Ben's office and dropped dead from a heart attack; and the next morning the accountants walked in and sacked Ben on the spot.

After that, he worked in Spain for Fred Pontin, then ran a pub in Chichester. Now he does his black-faced singing act again. In a way, Ben's career has come full circle.

The last time I saw him he was his usual ebullient self, telling me about all the work he had in hand ranging from old-time music hall at Clacton to panto at Torquay. Life was treating him well and I was happy for him.

I have been lucky to have met some extraordinary people who have become lasting friends: John Galvin, Peter Jackson, Ben of course and Vince Powell. I would do anything for any one of them and by the same token I get very melancholy if anyone I like lets me down.

All these friendships are with men. This is quite deliberate. After the sexual part of my marriage ended, I put a metaphorical brick wall between myself and women. I have a great respect and deep love for my wife. She came up the hard way with me. When we were first married, we lived in stinking twenty-five-bob-a-week combined rooms but she never complained. She worked hard and gave me a son whom I love dearly and I believe that if you take on marriage—or any commitment—then it is a duty to carry it through. So I will not take the risk of even a friendly, platonic relationship with a woman in case it might develop into something which would threaten my marriage.

There have, of course, been opportunities. There was a blonde bi-sexual singer—how about that?—who made it perfectly clear what she wanted. She even rang me at three in the morning with my wife asleep beside me. I hung up.

On the balance sheet, I think I have come out in the black. There have been regrets of course.

Occasionally, for example, I wonder what it would have been like to be a millionaire. It's not an idle thought. Twice I had the opportunity but my judgment was wrong. In 1957 Lew Grade asked me whether I had twenty thousand pounds. I said I had. He then tried to convince me to buy twenty thousand one pound shares in ATV, but I didn't go for it. I had no faith in commercial television. I thought that the future lay with a second BBC channel. So my reply was thanks but no thanks. Eighteen months later the shares were worth twenty-five pounds.

Then there was John Galvin who wanted me to invest in his mining and metal company but I turned him down. I could have been a millionaire twice over if I'd made the right decisions on those occasions; but there's no point in being smart in retrospect. You make your decisions and live with them.

In my career, though, I've been extremely fortunate. I have been privileged to work with some of the nicest and most talented people in the 'legitimate' theatre and TV. Scripts get delivered to my door and I give each one very careful consideration, although I've no ambition to do Shakespeare. I'd be no good with the language. I even had difficulty learning Shaw when I played 'Pygmalion'. I need to use contemporary language

One of my ambitions is to turn a Neville Shute novel, *The Pied Piper*, into a TV series. It's the story of a sixty-five-year-old Englishman who gets stranded in France at the outbreak of war and is asked by a French family to take their children back to England. As he crosses the country he collects kids until he has a whole tribe of them. I would like to do that, and I'd like to do anything new that was as good as 'Comedians'; but there's no great void in my life, no burning ambition to do anything other than good work.

I'm content. I'll know when to stop. When I start having trouble with my lines, I'll know. I won't need a director or a critic to tell me. If I became an embarrassment to myself or, more important, to other people, then it would be time, in the words of Jewel and Warriss's first TV series, to 'Turn It Up'.

But not yet ...

110 05